Believe in HER

Believe in HER

Why Girls Need Confidence and How to Cultivate It

DILJEET DOSANJH TAYLOR

BELIEVE IN HER
Why Girls Need Confidence and How to Cultivate It

Interior Layout and Design by Stephanie Anderson
Book Cover Design by Abigael Elliott
Cover Artwork by Eva Timothy
(www.evatimothy.com | IG: @eva_timothy)

ISBNs:
979-8-89165-156-2 *Paperback*
979-8-89165-157-9 *Hardback*
979-8-89165-155-5 *E-book*

Published by:
Streamline Books
Kansas City, MO
streamlinebookspublishing.com

To my boys, Taj and Avi, you've rewritten my story.

To my mom, grandma (Beji), and Aunt Rani for showing me that not all superheroes look like men.

To the little girl in all the women I've been blessed to coach, thank you for letting me believe in her.

To Frank Gagliano—Coach Gags—thank you for believing in me.

To the next generation of HER.

CONTENTS

INTRODUCTION

FOR OVER TWENTY years, I have stood on the sidelines (literally on the sidelines), cheering young women on as a coach and mentor. And there are things that remain just as true today as they were on my first day of coaching: As a society, we are failing our young women. Instead of a culture of confidence and empowerment, our young women are faced with scrutiny, judgment, and expectations at every turn. It's time something changed; it's time we changed the story.

In a world that often tells girls how they should be seen and heard, where their worth is too often tied to their appearance, and where they are expected to conform to societal ideals rather than embrace their true selves, it is no wonder that countless girls struggle to find their voice, believe in their abilities, and stand tall with confidence. The challenges they face are not simply a result of individual shortcomings but are deeply rooted in the insidious biases and expectations perpetuated by our culture, media, and even well-meaning individuals.

Growing up as a girl in a Punjabi immigrant house, I envied American girls. It seemed that they could do whatever they wanted, wear whatever they wanted, and *be* whoever they wanted. Their path seemed powerful and limitless, while mine was predetermined with a visible ceiling. However, I soon realized that the limited feeling and confidence struggles had less to do with being a *Punjabi girl* and more to do with just *being a girl* trying to grow up in a world structured mostly for men. In that sense, we were all growing up with the same pressures.

Throughout my journey as a coach, I have been a firsthand witness to the profound impact that a lack of confidence can have on the lives of girls. It becomes evident in the way they receive feedback, and it becomes apparent how the early years of adolescence, when puberty sets in, shape their self-perception. Their beliefs about their own potential, goals, intelligence, appearance, and preferences are all affected. I have observed talented athletes hesitating on the track, doubting their own abilities, and brilliant minds shrinking in group settings, afraid to speak up or share their ideas. I have seen women excessively apologize when seeking help, struggle to make eye contact when receiving compliments, freeze in situations where they should be advocating for themselves, settle for undeserving relationships, and simply crumble when faced with situations that require confidence.

It is heartbreaking to witness the potential of so many bright, talented, and capable girls and young women go unrealized because of a lack of confidence. And yet, it is not enough to simply acknowledge the problem; we must actively work to dismantle the barriers that hinder girls' belief in themselves and provide them with the tools and support system they need to thrive.

In this book, *Believe in HER*, I aim to address the insufficient awareness surrounding the biological, cultural, and societal differences between girls and boys, particularly during the crucial adolescent years. It is a call to action to support adolescent girls in developing healthy relationships, interpersonal beliefs, and self-confidence. We must recognize that girls experience unique challenges as they navigate the transition from childhood to adolescence and beyond. Biological differences, such as hormonal changes, can impact their behaviors, emotions, and the ways they perceive themselves and the world around them. Cultural and societal expectations further compound these challenges, placing undue pressure on girls to conform to narrow ideals of beauty, behavior, and achievement.

One of the challenges we face is the lack of accessible information on supporting girls' growth and confidence development. While there are resources available, they often fall short of providing actionable strategies that can make a real difference in the lives of girls. We need to bridge this gap and explore better approaches to instilling self-confidence in girls.

Believing in oneself is a transformative power that can shape lives and open doors to countless opportunities. By instilling self-belief and encouraging girls to take risks, we can empower them to overcome obstacles and reach their full potential.

My personal experience as a coach, mother, and woman has fueled my motivation to help adolescent girls. I have witnessed the incredible transformations that occur when girls are given the tools and support they need to believe in themselves. And now, I want to share my experiences in hopes of helping you do the same.

Through the pages of this book, we will delve into the challenges faced by girls and examine the underlying causes. We will explore the influential role of relationships, the power of belief, and the importance of gratitude and instilling confidence in others. We will encourage girls to dream big and envision a bold future for themselves.

It's time to rewrite the narrative for our young girls and create a world where they can thrive with confidence, authenticity, and resilience. Together, let's embark on this journey of empowering the next generation of strong, confident, and self-assured women.

Join me as we dive into the heart of *Believe in HER* and discover the power of instilling self-confidence in adolescent girls. Let us challenge the status quo, challenge the expectations placed upon girls, and create a new paradigm where every girl can truly believe in herself and her limitless potential.

The future of our world

is only as bright as the

future of our girls.

—MICHELLE OBAMA

CHAPTER 1

Embracing HER Journey

WHEN I WAS a fairly new college coach, I was asked to present at a high school coaches clinic. The topic was "Gender Effective Coaching." To be honest, I had to refer to Google to figure out exactly what I was supposed to talk about, and I quickly realized that I would be presenting on the differences in coaching boys and girls, or young men and young women.

At the time, I was one of the few females coaching both young men and young women on a college track team. I knew that I talked to male and female athletes differently, but I didn't really know why or what the impact was. I didn't want to come into this speaking engagement unprepared, so I did my research. I carefully combed through studies and videos, and I ended up falling down a swirling hole of the biological differences between males and females. And it was shocking.

Psychological statistics were perhaps the most startling—and the most pivotal—to me as a coach. What I found in my research, and what I have continued to find since that pivotal moment, is that from a young age, boys and girls are hardwired differently.

Decoding HER Differences

Puberty

The differences between boys and girls permeate our conversations, expectations, and even our subconscious responses as parents, coaches, teachers, or mentors. Sometimes, we may not even realize it, but it's there. You've probably heard those remarks like, "Oh, she's just more mature," or the classic, "Girls tend to outperform boys in school." And you know what? There's actually some scientific basis to it.

Puberty is that inevitable phase in your child's life that you can't help but approach with a mix of anticipation and trepidation. Typically occurring between the ages of eight and twelve, it ushers in a whirlwind of psychological, hormonal, and physical changes. This is the "tween time"—a period when their voices take on different pitches, their bodies experience growth spurts, and pesky acne may make an appearance. For girls, it also marks the onset of menstruation, reminding you that it's probably time for that first bra-shopping trip.

Interestingly, studies reveal that girls tend to embark on this journey a tad earlier than boys.[1] You might notice this discrepancy around sixth grade when the girls often tower over their male counterparts and unmistakably display signs of puberty. It may take a few more years for the boys to return from their summer breaks suddenly several inches taller.

While it may seem like a trivial detail, the fact that girls hit puberty first holds significant implications for their future. This early milestone sets the stage for the trajectory of their lives, influencing various aspects, from their physical development to their social and emotional well-being.

The Prefrontal Cortex

Puberty is an incredible time when girls experience something pretty amazing—their brains go into overdrive. During puberty, girls' prefrontal cortexes—the part of the brain responsible for shaping our personality—develop faster than boys'. It's like they're sprinting ahead in the race of brain maturation, reaching full development by the age of twenty-four.[2]

But why does this matter? The prefrontal cortex helps us respond to things around us, manage emotions, make decisions, and navigate the tricky world of social interactions. So, when girls' prefrontal cortexes develop faster, they find themselves processing and reacting to the world, the environments they're in, and all the pressures and expectations that come their way at an earlier age. To say it's a lot for them to handle would be an understatement.

And there's more to it. During puberty, girls' brains get a hormone boost—estrogen takes the stage. Now, estrogen has been linked to higher rates of depression, and this hormonal surge can show itself in different ways, affecting their emotional well-being.[3] If you're a parent, you will likely observe moodiness, sudden changes in behavior, or even some more alarming side effects of estrogen. It's like a dance between biology and the world around them, and it's crucial for us to recognize and understand these factors as we support and guide girls through this new phase of their lives.

The impact of girls developing faster than boys goes beyond just physical changes. It's about how they rapidly respond to the world, the environment they find themselves in, and all the pressures and expectations that come their way at a much earlier age. As parents, educators, and mentors, it's essential for us to be aware of these dynamics and create a nurturing and understanding environment for girls as they embark on this accelerated journey of growth and self-discovery.

As girls go through all the wild changes happening in their bodies and brains, they're also dealing with a lot of other stuff. Think about it—they're trying to figure out who they are, make friends, do well in school, compete in sports, and just be human beings. And let's be real: It's a ton of stress.

When we zoom out and look at the big picture, it totally makes sense why girls struggle with things like being afraid to fail, feeling self-conscious about their bodies, always wanting to please people, and lacking confidence. We, as parents, mentors, teachers, and coaches, often see it as just a tough phase that they have to get through. But what if we could understand why our young women face these challenges before they grow up? What if we could change the story and help our daughters, athletes, and students avoid the common traps of the tween years? In order to help, we first have to get to the heart of the issue.

Identifying HER Struggles

Fear of Failure

The prefrontal cortex of the brain is responsible for decision-making, impulse control, and emotional regulation. And since the prefrontal cortex develops faster in girls, they often exhibit greater levels of caution and worry, opting for more conservative approaches when faced with risky situations.[4] Unfortunately, societal norms and expectations can exacerbate these differences.

Society often perpetuates the idea that risk-taking is a more desirable trait in boys while praising their failures as valuable learning experiences. In contrast, girls are frequently subjected to higher expectations and an emphasis on avoiding failure. From a young age, they are socialized to believe that failure is something to be feared and avoided at all costs. This societal conditioning can lead to feelings of insecurity and self-doubt among girls, causing them to hold back from taking risks and settle for outcomes that are perceived as "good enough" to meet the expectations placed upon them.

In one of my favorite books, *The Confidence Code for Girls*, the BBC World News Washington correspondent and news anchor Katty Kay and senior national correspondent for *Good Morning America* Claire Shipman revealed their findings from a study conducted with Ypulse, which shows that between the ages of twelve and thirteen, the percentage of girls who say they're not allowed to fail increases by 150 percent.[5] Yes, you read that right, one hundred and fifty percent. Clearly, something is happening in these pivotal years of adolescence that trains girls that failure is wrong, or at the very least, not okay. So, they continue through their years of adolescence, dropping out of sports they may be good at, quitting clubs they enjoy, and generally feeling like failing is not an option. And as parents, teachers, and coaches, we perpetuate this by praising the outcomes far more than the effort it took to reach those outcomes.

In the early years of developing confidence, *it is extremely important to praise the process and the work regardless of the outcome.* It is an unattainable expectation of perfection that our young girls are carrying on their backs. We must focus on the process of trying rather than focusing on the result.

A few years ago, my son won the sixth-grade spelling bee. I was proud, and I felt full of joy for his accomplishment. For the next few weeks, I said things like, "I'm so proud of you for winning the spelling bee!" and I walked around the house, yelling, "Spelling bee champion!" When I was growing up, I had won my sixth-grade spelling bee, and it felt like a special bond I could have with my son—we were both champions. As a coach and a mom, it's a delicate balance to celebrate results but also to applaud the effort. I've done it numerous times with athletes who are already hyperfocused on winning. I've done it numerous times with my own children with grades and basketball games. I have to be super intentional about reminding myself to applaud how hard they work rather than what the outcome is.

When I reflected on this later, I realized that I was praising the *outcome* instead of the *effort*. Sure, he'd won the spelling bee. And that was cool. But do you know what was way cooler? The effort he put in to get there: the late nights sitting on the barstool in the kitchen reviewing word after word after word; the moments when he asked me to quiz him before school or after school; the way he probably fell asleep silently spelling out words night after night. The effort was what mattered, the work he put in to get to where he wanted to be.

If I could go back, I would say more things like, "I am so proud of the work you did to get here," or simply support him better along the process. So often, parents, coaches, and teachers (just like me!) praise the outcome instead of the effort. *Oh, you got an A on the test! Well done!* Instead of *Wow, I know you've been working so hard on this. I am proud of you!* These may be unintentional slip-ups, but words matter. And for our girls, they indicate that not meeting the expectations set for them equals failure, and failure equals displeasure or punishment.

We have to do better. We have to frame perceived failures in a way that empowers our young girls to try, try harder, and try again. Even if every single outcome looks like a "failure," imagine the growth that comes from the process of trying. We can and should celebrate outcomes by praising the effort. We need to change our own views on failure, how we talk about failures, and how we set expectations for our girls. We need to support them in the whole process instead of just in the result.

Body Image

A study conducted by the Mental Health Foundation found that 46 percent of adolescent girls are more likely to worry "often" or "always" about their body image, compared to 25 percent of adolescent boys.[6] Regrettably, these percentages only escalate as individuals progress through the stages of life, reaching a crescendo of distress that persists until approximately forty years of age, when men and women reach similar levels of confidence.

The implications of this pervasive issue extend far beyond the confines of mere self-perception. Adolescent girls, burdened by the weight of societal expectations, find themselves navigating treacherous waters where their participation in sports, extracurricular activities, and even their interpersonal relationships are significantly impacted. From a tender age, girls are subjected to the relentless indoctrination of societal norms—regardless of their familial environment—which dictates that their primary worth lies in conforming to narrow standards of beauty. As a society, we continue to grapple with the alarming prevalence of eating disorders and other mental health disorders that impact increasingly younger and younger adolescents and children. But we created and perpetuate the problem! In essence, we are unwittingly shaping the future of our young girls, instilling in them the belief that their self-worth is intrinsically tied to their external appearance.

The notion of "pretty privilege" may make you laugh, but the consequences are anything but humorous, particularly for our vulnerable young girls. Unconsciously driven by the fear of falling short of society's idealized beauty standards, they harbor deep-seated apprehensions about their desirability and the potential ramifications of failing to meet these unattainable criteria. A glance at the magazine covers adorning grocery store shelves or a mere thirty-second scroll through the seemingly infinite realm of Instagram is all it takes to witness the ways our society idolizes a flawless, unrealistic standard of beauty. And if it impacts adults, think of how much more it impacts your daughter, your athletes, or your students.

Dove recently launched an inspiring campaign called the Dove Self-Esteem Project that aims to tackle the issue of confidence and body image among girls. You might have come across their commercials during March Madness, but let me break it down for you. Dove has invested years of research into understanding the dynamics of confidence, body image, and girls' participation in sports.

To take their efforts a step further, Dove has developed educational materials designed to help coaches and parents better comprehend what their daughters are going through. They want to provide support and guidance in a way that empowers girls to navigate these challenges with a strong sense of self-esteem.

One remarkable study conducted by Dove in collaboration with Nike gave birth to the campaign #KeepHerConfident in Sports. The findings from these two influential companies were eye-opening—a staggering 45 percent of girls quit sports by the age of fourteen due to low body confidence.[7] This statistic is truly striking. When I first read it, I was taken aback. But upon reflection, it starts to make sense.

Think about all the times you've heard girls and women you know make comments about not liking how they look in a swimsuit, a leotard, spandex, or even just shorts. The truth is these negative feelings about their appearance can erode their confidence and make them uncomfortable participating in sports. It's not surprising, then, that girls might give up on sports altogether if they don't feel good about themselves.

People-Pleasing

In *The Confidence Code,* the authors dive even deeper into their study and reveal that between their tween (nine to twelve years old) and teen years (thirteen to eighteen years old), girls' confidence that other people like them falls from 71 percent (yes, people like me) to 38 percent (I worry that others don't like me).[8] That is a 46 percent drop in just a few years' time. The question naturally arises: What transpires during this time period that triggers such a dramatic decline in girls' belief that they are genuinely liked or accepted by others? As our girls navigate the intricate labyrinth of teenagehood, an unexpected wave of self-doubt crashes upon them, intensifying their anxiety and fostering an increasing concern that they may not be truly valued or embraced by their peers. This apprehension takes root and sprouts into a tendency toward people-pleasing—a desire to do whatever it takes to win the favor and approval of others, regardless of it being at the risk of their own authenticity.

For some girls, people-pleasing may manifest as an incessant need to smile more, wear makeup, or conform to the norms and expectations of their social circles in order to "fit in." Others may seek validation through academic or athletic achievements, eagerly craving the affirmation and attention of their admirers. Meanwhile, a subset of girls might set impossibly high standards for themselves, driven by the belief that only by surpassing these expectations can they attain the affirmation and care they yearn for so deeply. Their self-worth is being framed by how well they are liked or how good they are at things. Rather than simply being of value, they feel forced to bring their value in a way that impresses others.

Sometimes, we don't realize it, but the pressure to please others starts right at home, especially for girls. Our families may have expectations for us, and we might feel like we have to meet those expectations to make them happy. We worry about disappointing our loved ones or doing things just to get their approval. It's like we're always trying to live up to these standards that aren't even our own.

Navigating this situation can be tough because we can't completely get rid of expectations at home. But what we can do is make sure those expectations come from a place of genuine belief. When expectations don't align with what we truly believe about ourselves, they become empty and unfulfilling. We end up feeling like we're not good enough and keep trying to please others.

But here's the thing: We can change this pattern. We can create home environments where expectations are reasonable and support is constant. It's about having open and honest conversations with our parents or guardians, where we can share our thoughts and feelings without fearing judgment. It's about them recognizing and appreciating our unique strengths, talents, and interests. They should encourage us to be ourselves and not just focus on what others think of us.

Setting realistic expectations that match our abilities is important too. We should be allowed to make mistakes, learn from them, and grow. It's not just about the end result but also about the effort we put in and the lessons we learn along the way.

In our homes, we should have the freedom to explore different activities and pursue our passions. When we're given the chance to take risks, make decisions, and learn from both successes and failures, we become more confident in ourselves. It's about finding our own paths and believing in our abilities.

By creating supportive and accepting home environments that value our individuality and encourage us to be true to ourselves, we can break free from the constant need to please others. It won't happen overnight, but with time, patience, and support, we can become strong and confident young women who follow our own dreams and live life on our own terms.

Confidence

At the core of an adolescent girl's—or, in fact, any human's—fear of failure, inclination to people-please, struggles with body image, and various other challenges lies a fundamental ingredient: confidence. It serves as the bedrock upon which our sense of self is built, and its absence can have far-reaching consequences. According to a report from the Ypulse research group and the authors of *The Confidence Code for Girls*, between ages eight and fourteen, girl's confidence levels drop by 30 percent.[9]

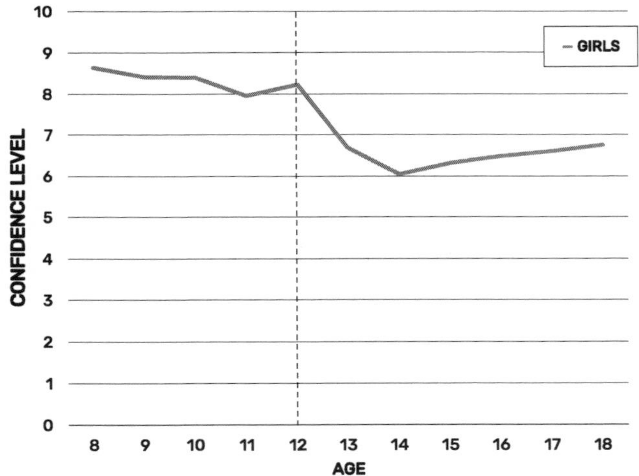

Results based on Ypulse survey research conducted Feb 8th - Feb 13th, 2018 among 864 girls aged 8-18.

What is even more startling is that this confidence gap does not balance out until around age forty.[10]

The decline in confidence among young girls is a big concern. When they don't feel confident, self-doubt sneaks into their minds and alters how they see themselves. You might hear them say things like, "I can't do that because I'm not tall enough," or, "I'm not smart enough." It's sad to see their once vibrant spirits fade away, and they start to hide who they really are.

This lack of confidence affects many parts of their lives. It affects how they do in school, how they relate to others, and how they feel overall. Without confidence, they're afraid to take risks, and their dreams get put on hold. They can't fully embrace their own potential.

This confidence gap has serious consequences. Adolescence should be a time of self-discovery, growth, and feeling empowered. But for many girls, it becomes a battle where their confidence gets chipped away, leaving them feeling vulnerable and unprepared for life's challenges.

We need to recognize and do something about this troubling reality. It's up to all of us—parents, teachers, mentors, and society as a whole—to create environments where girls' confidence can flourish. We need to change the stories we tell and promote self-acceptance, resilience, and the celebration of different talents and abilities.

Parents, educators, and mentors have special roles in building girls' confidence. We need to give them the tools to bounce back from setbacks, create supportive communities, and focus on more than appearances and achievements. By doing this, we can start closing the confidence gap and help girls grow into strong and self-assured young women who can take on anything.

The Impact

The impact of confidence, or the lack thereof, affects various aspects of a young girl's life. When I coached both genders, I often had combined practices and team meetings. Anytime I made generalized statements about what we should be doing better, the women would walk away from the meeting or practice carrying the blame for a lack of effort or commitment. This was the part of my career where I started having individual meetings to provide feedback and did less generalized coaching. The men would leave these combined meetings unbothered or fazed, and the women would often be close to tears, feeling like they didn't measure up to the standards of success for themselves. It was startling to see the way each gender processed feedback.

These tendencies are interconnected. When a girl lacks confidence, it often leads to people-pleasing, fear of failure, and negative body image becoming more pronounced. Have you met a young girl or a woman who apologizes for everything or is constantly anxious that someone is mad at her? It comes from a lack of confidence. If we invest in building our daughters' confidence at ages nine, ten, eleven, and twelve, it will make a huge difference in their lives when they're nineteen, twenty, twenty-one, and beyond.

Confidence, or the lack of it, has a lasting impact on girls. It affects their academic pursuits, career choices, relationships, and how they see themselves. A confident girl can face challenges with resilience, embrace her unique identity, and pursue her dreams. On the other hand, a lack of confidence creates barriers that hold her back from reaching her full potential and living a fulfilling life.

To sum up, confidence plays a significant role in young girls' lives. It influences how they respond to criticism, take on blame, and engage in people-pleasing, fear of failure, and negative body image. If we invest in building their confidence early on, we can help them thrive and succeed as they grow. Adolescent girls without dreams become women without clear vision. But girls with dreams become women with vision. We want our daughters, our friends, our athletes, and our students to become women with vision.

Think about It

1. What questions can we ask girls and young women that will help them focus on the things they like about themselves instead of their perceived flaws?

2. How can we create an inclusive environment where girls feel supported and encouraged to participate in sports, activities, and leadership, no matter how they look or their talents?

Be about It

Foster open conversations: Initiate discussions about body image, encouraging self-love and acceptance to create a safe space for girls to express their thoughts.

Teach media literacy: Empower girls to critically analyze media messages, question unrealistic beauty standards, and develop a discerning perspective.

Promote inclusivity and mentorship: Advocate for equal opportunities and supportive policies that encourage girls' participation in sports, extracurricular activities, and leadership roles while providing mentorship and role models to guide and inspire them.

It's not about being

the 'first' or the 'only'...

it's about creating a

pathway for the girls

coming up.

—JUSTINE SIEGAL

CHAPTER 2

Why Do Girls Struggle with Confidence?

WHEN I STARTED kindergarten, I did not speak any English. I couldn't understand what the teacher was saying or what she expected from me. I didn't know what my fellow classmates meant, how to make friends, or how to act in a classroom setting. Yes, I learned very quickly, but before I learned English, I learned how to smile. I smiled most of the day because I noticed, when I sat with a smile, even without speaking, my teacher and classmates would smile back at me. So when someone told me to do something, I just smiled until I could figure out what they were trying to say.

Naturally, I quickly turned into the "girl with the smile" because it was—quite literally—the only thing I felt confident doing. I became the girl in class who was happy but didn't know how to speak English. And even though I now speak English very well, smiling is still my default, all because of my experience in elementary school. In the same way, so much of the behavior and struggles we see in young girls today are trained and ingrained into them starting in elementary school.

This struggle is a mix of different things—it's influenced by biological differences, societal norms, and cultural expectations. It's complicated, and it's important for us to understand it. By uncovering the factors that contribute to this struggle, we can start empowering girls to defy those limitations and build their confidence.

Hormones

Throughout my conversations with numerous parents of young women over the years, a common frustration emerged—a perplexing sense of bewilderment regarding the changes that occur in girls between the ages of eight and twelve. While it is widely acknowledged that the teenage years can be challenging, there is a wealth of hidden complexities that unfold during the preteen stage, and hormones play a significant role in this period.

Many of my women have identified these adolescent years as the phase of life where they started struggling with confidence. Some of it had to do with their bodies changing, and oftentimes, comments made to them by coaches or parents caused them to fight to keep their prepubescent bodies rather than embrace their development into womanhood. Some of the comments came from peers and friends, which directly impacted how they felt about themselves. And this doesn't include the silent messages repeated to them through social media, making them feel that they were not enough as they are. As we discussed in chapter 1, girls experience a surge of estrogen—the primary female sex hormone—during this time, triggering a cascade of physical and emotional changes. All of these things, combined with no proper way to navigate these newfound feelings, leave our girls in a state of confusion.

In comparison, boys experience a surge of testosterone—the primary male sex hormone—during their own journeys through puberty. While testosterone shares some similarities with estrogen, there are key differences in the timing and effects of these hormones. Girls tend to experience puberty earlier than boys, primarily due to the earlier rise of estrogen. This difference in timing accounts for the mental and emotional disparities that girls may encounter during the tween years. You've probably heard that when boys hit puberty, they get bigger, stronger, taller, and faster. On the opposite side, it is often assumed that girls tend to get more emotional, sensitive, and aware of how people feel about them during puberty. And while puberty impacts every child differently, the stereotypes can generally be considered true.

The impact of estrogen extends far beyond simply the physical changes a girl experiences. As girls navigate the turbulent waters of their tween years, this hormone exerts a profound influence on their emotional and psychological landscapes. The surge of estrogen can lead to heightened emotions, intensified mood swings, and an increased sensitivity to social interactions. It is as if their internal world is in a constant state of flux, often leaving both girls and their parents feeling bewildered and frustrated.

The interplay between hormones and emotions becomes particularly noticeable during this stage. Girls may find themselves experiencing joy, sadness, anger, and anxiety in rapid succession, sometimes without a clear understanding of why. It is crucial for parents and caregivers to recognize that these emotional fluctuations are a normal part of the developmental process, driven by the intricate dance of hormones within their child's body.

The tween years also mark a period of self-discovery and identity formation. Girls begin to explore who they are and where they fit into the world. Estrogen, acting in conjunction with other hormones, plays a pivotal role in shaping their senses of self and their emerging identities. It is during this time that girls may start to question their appearance, compare themselves to others, and grapple with body image concerns. These internal struggles can have profound impacts on their confidence and self-belief. In modern-day America, is it any wonder our girls are struggling? They are bombarded by messaging that tells them they are not pretty enough, not athletic enough, not *good* enough. And when you add this to the already-difficult hormone changes, it takes girls who struggle with confidence and turns them into women who struggle with confidence.

Societal Expectations (Be a "Good Girl")

Society has long perpetuated a narrative that places unrealistic expectations on girls while granting boys more freedom to be themselves. You may have heard phrases like "boys will be boys," which implies that boys have more freedom to engage in certain behaviors without judgment or consequences. They are typically given leeway to be more rambunctious and assertive and to make mistakes.

However, young women are rarely provided with the same freedoms and are often conditioned to strive for perfection and fit into predefined molds. They are expected to be quiet, compliant, and conform to societal standards. As psychologist Susan Albers discusses in "6 Signs You Have 'Good Girl Syndrome,'" good-girl syndrome is the "manifestation of traits that are valued or praised in girls." It's basically the idea that "good girls" are obedient, quiet, and pretty. She points out that it has a lot to do with how caregivers interact with girls when they are young that shapes what they expect of themselves and, ultimately, who they become. And as I think we can all agree, she concludes that good-girl syndrome is a problem that leads to people-pleasing, perfectionism, and negative body image.[11]

If you haven't watched the movie *Barbie*, directed by Greta Gerwig, there is a fantastic portion where Barbie expresses the conflicting messages women are constantly bombarded with. It made women feel seen and heard and deeply resonated with women across the country. It sounds like this:

> It is literally impossible to be a woman. You are so beautiful, and so smart, and it kills me that you don't think you're good enough. Like we always have to be extraordinary, but somehow, we're always doing it wrong. You have to be thin but not too thin. You have to say you

want to be healthy, but you also have to be thin. You have to have money, but you can't ask for money because that's crass. You have to be a boss, but you can't be mean. You have to lead but you can't squash other people's ideas. You're supposed to love being a mother but don't talk about your kids all the d*** time. You have to be a career woman but also always be looking out for other people. You have to answer for men's bad behavior, which is insane, but if you point that out, you're accused of complaining. You're supposed to stay pretty for men, but not so pretty that you tempt them too much or that you threaten other women because you're supposed to be part of the sisterhood. But always stand out and always be grateful. But never forget the system is rigged. So find a way to acknowledge that but also always be grateful. You have to never get old, never be rude, never show off, never be selfish, never fall down, never fail, never show fear, never get out of line. It's too hard! It's too contradictory, and nobody gives you a medal or says thank you! And it turns out in fact that not only are you doing everything wrong, but also everything is your fault.[12]

At its core, the societal expectations imposed upon women are crippling. Instead of nurturing their individuality and teaching them to advocate for themselves, society trains them to be products of its desires. It stifles their true potential and limits their growth. The pressure to conform prevents them from fully expressing themselves and reaching their true potential.

The consequences of these expectations are profound. Women are denied the opportunity to advocate for themselves, assert their needs, and challenge the status quo. Their achievements often go unrecognized, and their aspirations are limited. This lack of empowerment and recognition undermines their self-confidence and hinders their personal and professional growth. It is crucial to break free from these patterns and cultivate a society that encourages girls and women to embrace their uniqueness, pursue their passions, and assert themselves.

To create meaningful change, we must challenge and redefine societal norms. Celebrating the diversity of experiences, talents, and aspirations among girls and women is essential. By dismantling the "good-girl" paradigm, we can empower girls and women by providing them with the tools, support, and opportunities to pursue their dreams, challenge stereotypes, and contribute to society on their own terms.

But how do we do that? It's not something that will disappear overnight. But by creating space to have intentional conversations with our girls, we can take a step in the right direction.

We can create spaces where our girls and young women feel supported simply by listening. Listen to the pressures they feel. Ask them questions, and then listen. Then you can offer advice based on your own experiences. At the end of the day, our girls need support. They need to know they are not alone, and they need to have role models to look up to, women who have defied societal norms and broken through the glass ceiling.

It is time to create a society that uplifts and empowers girls and women. By embracing their individuality and providing equal opportunities, we can break free from the constraints of societal expectations. Let us reimagine a world where young girls can grow up confident in their abilities, unburdened by contradictory expectations, and empowered to shape their own destinies.

Social Media

Filters

Filters. They're everywhere in our world today. Social media has made them a common tool, allowing us to change our looks with a simple swipe or tap. These digital tricks have completely transformed how we present ourselves online, creating a virtual reality where it's easy to look perfect with just a filter.

Filters give us all sorts of options. We can smooth out our skin, brighten our eyes, reshape our faces, and even change our hair color. And some digital tools can even be used to change your body. Think of the latest edition of *Sports Illustrated: Swimsuit Edition.* Do you think women really look like that? They are airbrushed to perfection, hiding anything that looks unflattering. Filters let us match up to the beauty standards society sets, even if those standards seem impossible in real life. With a few tweaks, we can erase our flaws and show the world a flawless version of who we are.

But filters have a big impact on young women's confidence and self-esteem. Seeing all those digitally altered images messes with their idea of beauty and makes them believe they need to be something they're not. They feel inadequate and constantly strive for an ideal that's just not real. And if you don't believe me, just take a look at the alarming rise in body dissatisfaction, eating disorders, and mental health issues among young women. The constant exposure to filtered and photoshopped images creates an unattainable standard of beauty that leaves many feeling like they don't measure up. In 2021, ParentsTogether conducted a survey on the use of social media filters. In the study, 61 percent of teens said that the use of filters made them feel worse about how they looked in real life.[13]

The pressure to conform to these unrealistic beauty standards takes a toll on girls and women. They start questioning their own worth and value based on how closely they resemble the filtered and edited images they see online. The desire to be "perfect" becomes all-consuming, leading to a never-ending cycle of self-doubt and self-criticism. They may feel pressured to constantly compare themselves to others, seeking validation and approval in the form of likes, comments, and followers.

The Comparison Trap

You've probably noticed how social media can make young women feel worse about themselves. It's a place where they constantly compare themselves to others and strive to meet unrealistic standards. The carefully curated posts and filtered images create an illusion of perfection that can be hard to live up to.

Research tells us that spending too much time on social media can harm self-esteem. Girls and young women may find themselves constantly comparing their appearance to others and feeling unhappy with their bodies.[14] It's tough for them to recognize that what they see on social media isn't the whole story.

One significant factor in this comparison game is the influence of social media influencers.[15] These influencers, especially in the beauty industry, often present an unattainable standard of beauty. When young women follow them, they start believing that they should look just like them. It's essential for us to help them understand that true beauty comes in all shapes, sizes, and colors. Encourage them to embrace their unique qualities and celebrate their inner strengths.

Another challenge is the fear of missing out (FOMO).[16] As young women scroll through their feeds, they may see their peers having incredible experiences and achieving great things. It's easy to feel left out, or like they're not measuring up. We need to remind them that social media often showcases the highlights, not the everyday struggles and challenges. Encourage them to focus on their own journeys and celebrate their own accomplishments, no matter how big or small.

So, how can we help girls and young women navigate the social media maze? Firstly, let's open up the conversation. A teen's social media access should come with a parental set of guidelines and rules. Talk to them about the pressures they may be experiencing and listen to their concerns. Create a safe space where they feel comfortable discussing their feelings about social media. Discuss the dangers that are lurking in the online world. While there are some benefits to certain aspects of social media and online connection, there are a large amount of risks.

Next, help them develop healthy mindsets. Teach them to be critical consumers of social media content. Remind them that what they see online is often an idealized version of reality. Encourage them to focus on their own growth, talents, and passions rather than comparing themselves to others.

Additionally, guide them in curating their social media feeds. Encourage them to follow accounts that promote body positivity, self-acceptance, and empowerment. Help them recognize that their worth is not determined by the number of likes or followers they have. Real connections and genuine friendships matter more than virtual popularity.

Lastly, encourage a healthy balance between online and offline activities. Encourage them to engage in hobbies, sports, and face-to-face interactions. Remind them that there's a whole world beyond the screen waiting to be explored.

Cultural Expectations

Gender Norms

In many cultures, including American society, gender norms have long been established for men and women. These norms often dictate specific roles and expectations, placing women in the position of marrying, having children, taking care of the household chores, and finding fulfillment in these traditional roles. This can be a touchy subject based on religion and upbringing, and I realize that some individuals genuinely find happiness and fulfillment in these roles, but the problem arises when these expectations become generalized and imposed upon all women.

Historically, women in America were expected to adhere to strict societal expectations, often influenced by religious beliefs. They were encouraged to marry at a young age, prioritize family over personal aspirations, and dedicate themselves to maintaining the household. However, during World War II, the absence of men in the workforce created an opportunity for women to step into traditionally male-dominated roles and contribute to the war effort. Women joined the workforce, handled various responsibilities, and demonstrated their capability to juggle multiple roles simultaneously.

The end of the war marked a shift in societal attitudes. Advertisements and cultural messaging aimed to encourage women to return to domestic life, promoting images of the ideal housewife engaged in cooking and utilizing household appliances. While some women willingly embraced this return to traditional gender roles, others found it difficult to relinquish the newfound independence and agency they had experienced during the war.

This period of social change paved the way for the women's rights movement and the pursuit of equal rights and opportunities. However, despite significant progress and advancements, the perception of success and power continues to be predominantly associated with men in our modern world. When girls are exposed to a social environment where women are portrayed as lacking autonomy and control over their lives, they internalize these limitations and may struggle to envision a future where they can pursue their aspirations fully.

As parents, teachers, coaches, and examples for young women, we need to challenge these cultural expectations and foster an environment that empowers girls and women to believe in their abilities and potential. By providing them with positive role models who demonstrate agency and success, we can help dismantle the notion that success is solely driven by men. Encouraging girls to explore diverse career paths, promoting education and skill development, and emphasizing the value of personal agency can help break the cycle of limited expectations and inspire them to pursue their passions and goals.

The Damsel in Distress

The concept of the damsel in distress is deeply ingrained in many cultural narratives and societal expectations surrounding women. From a young age, girls are often exposed to messages that reinforce the idea that they need to be rescued or saved by someone else. Phrases like "One day your prince will come" or "Someday you'll get married and be able to stay home" perpetuate the notion that a woman's ultimate fulfillment and happiness depend on finding a partner who will provide for and protect her. Hopefully, the prince does come if she wants him to. Hopefully, she can get married and stay home if she wants to. But let it be a choice rather than a requirement.

These messages can have far-reaching consequences on a girl's sense of self-worth, aspirations, and autonomy. They imply that women are incomplete, lacking agency, and in need of external validation or support. By instilling this belief from an early age, we unintentionally limit girls' aspirations, discourage their pursuit of independence, and reinforce the notion that their value lies primarily in their relationships with others.

Such messaging also reinforces traditional gender roles and expectations, where women are often portrayed as passive, dependent, and submissive. It creates a power imbalance and perpetuates the idea that women should prioritize their roles as caregivers, homemakers, and nurturers rather than pursuing their own ambitions and dreams. This isn't saying women can't be completely fulfilled by motherhood because I believe they can, as long as it is a choice and not an expectation.

It is crucial to challenge these narratives and instead empower girls to develop strong senses of self, independence, and resilience. By encouraging them to explore their own interests, pursue education, and develop skills that foster self-reliance, we can help them break free from the limitations imposed by the damsel-in-distress trope.

Promoting messages that emphasize self-determination, personal growth, and the pursuit of individual passions can inspire girls to envision a future where their happiness and fulfillment are not contingent upon finding a romantic partner or conforming to societal expectations.

Familial Expectations

Growing up in a Punjabi household, I experienced firsthand the profound impact that familial expectations can have on a girl's upbringing. It became evident to me from the very beginning that there was a stark contrast between the celebratory atmosphere surrounding the birth of a boy and the apologetic tone associated with the birth of a girl. This cultural dynamic served as a poignant reminder of the deeply entrenched gender bias that persisted within our society, a bias that unfortunately often continues to influence lives well into adulthood.

The way we structure our households and raise our children matters greatly. Whether we have boys or girls, a blended family, a single-parent home, or a two-parent home, the dynamics and expectations we establish within our homes leave a lasting impact. Our actions and behaviors as parents shape the beliefs, attitudes, and self-perceptions of our daughters, which in turn shape their lives for years to come.

Having had the opportunity to work closely with young women on a daily basis, I have personally witnessed the diverse range of backgrounds and experiences they come from. These experiences have given me a deeper understanding of the profound impact that familial expectations can have on a girl's development and journey toward adulthood. I have worked with women from various backgrounds, educated and uneducated, including religious and nonreligious households, as well as those from controlling or abusive environments. And if I could leave you with only one thing, I would reinforce that the way you structure your home has a profound and lasting impact on your children. Think about it, take the time to learn more, and give it everything you've got. Because, in a very real sense, our girls are counting on us.

Think about It

1. How can we encourage open and supportive communication within families to create a nurturing environment for girls to thrive and challenge societal constraints?

2. What strategies or initiatives do you believe can effectively promote gender equality within various cultural contexts?

3. How can we ensure that young women from diverse backgrounds, including those from controlling or abusive households, receive the necessary support and resources to overcome the challenges imposed by familial expectations?

Be about It

Educate yourself on what your daughter/athlete/student needs: Take the initiative to learn about the specific needs, challenges, and aspirations of the girls you are supporting. Listen to their perspectives, concerns, and goals, and seek resources or information that can help address those needs. By gaining a deeper understanding of their individual experiences, you can provide more effective support and guidance, fostering an environment where they can thrive and overcome societal constraints.

Emphasize internal compliments as opposed to external compliments: Emphasizing internal compliments over external compliments involves recognizing and appreciating personal qualities and achievements rather than solely focusing on outward appearance. For example, instead of complimenting a girl solely on how she looks, we can emphasize her intelligence, creativity, kindness, or resilience. By highlighting these internal qualities, we help girls develop a strong sense of self-worth based on their inherent strengths and abilities, fostering confidence and promoting a healthy self-image.

Promote gender equality within cultural contexts: Initiate cultural-awareness programs and dialogues that highlight the importance of gender equality and challenge traditional norms and stereotypes. Support initiatives that engage community leaders, educators, and influencers to promote inclusive practices, education, and equal opportunities for girls and young women within their cultural context.

Nothing can dim the light that shines from within.

—MAYA ANGELOU

CHAPTER 3

The Queen

THE GAME OF chess was a big deal in my house. It was a family tradition for my grandpa, dad, and older brother to play chess every day. But there was one thing that bothered me—I was originally never invited to join. Why? I assumed it was because I was a girl. The women in my family were not seen playing chess in the afternoons. They were expected to stick to the kitchen and household chores instead of playing games.

Even though I was originally excluded from the chess games, I was intrigued by the strategy and purpose. I would sit and watch from the corner of the couch or the brick seating of the fireplace, trying to learn the game. I observed my grandpa and brother strategizing and making moves on the chessboard. It took months, but I started to understand the basics. I learned which pieces were important and why sacrificing some was necessary to protect the king. It was ironic how the king just sat in the same square most of the time, kind of like the kings in my house.

One thing that caught my attention was the power and importance of the queen. In chess, the queen is like a superhero. She can move all over the board, capturing the enemy's pieces and posing a constant threat to the opponent's king. And once you lose the queen, you have a very minimal chance of winning the game. Watching those after-school chess matches, I realized that the queen symbolized both power and value. Because she brought such value to the game, she was coveted as the most powerful piece on the board. The queen was the first powerful woman I saw who had the ability to dominate in her role. It was an early lesson for me on the importance of power and value. I knew that as I grew up, I would need to bring high value to whatever board I was playing on.

Intrinsic Worth

For centuries, women have faced oppression, marginalization, and silencing all over the world. They have been treated as second-class citizens, lacking the same value and respect given to men in positions of power. Growing up, I internalized these beliefs and saw women being treated as somehow inferior. They were denied the recognition and respect that men with power received.

However, my observations of the chessboard and the significance of the queen made me question these notions. I realized that women, like the queen, possess intrinsic worth that is not defined by societal norms or power structures. Women bring unique qualities, strengths, and contributions that hold immense value. They have the potential to be powerful agents of change and catalysts for progress.

Recognizing and honoring the intrinsic worth of women is not just a matter of justice and equality; it is also essential for societal transformation. When women are valued and respected, society as a whole benefits. Their diverse perspectives, ideas, and talents can shape a more inclusive and vibrant world.

Imagine a world where women are given the recognition and respect they deserve. It's a world where their diverse perspectives, ideas, and talents are valued and embraced. In this world, everyone benefits.

Firstly, when women are valued and respected, it paves the way for gender equality. Equal treatment and opportunities for women lead to a fairer and more harmonious society. It means breaking down barriers and ensuring that women have the same chances as men in education, work, and leadership. When women can participate fully and have a say in shaping society, it creates a more just and inclusive world.

But it doesn't stop there. Women bring a wealth of unique perspectives to the table. Their varied experiences, influenced by factors like culture, background, and personal identity, offer fresh insights and alternative viewpoints. By embracing these diverse perspectives, we make our society stronger and more adaptable. We become better equipped to tackle complex challenges and find innovative solutions.

Valuing and respecting women is also essential for fostering creativity and innovation. When women are empowered to share their ideas and talents, it leads to a more vibrant intellectual landscape. Diverse teams that include women have been shown to generate more innovative ideas, solve problems more effectively, and drive economic growth. By empowering women and including them, we unlock a wellspring of creativity that benefits us all.

Valuing and respecting women means taking practical actions and changing societal attitudes. It starts with ensuring equal access to education, health care, and economic opportunities. When women have the same educational and economic prospects as men, they can achieve their full potential and positively impact their communities.

We also need to challenge gender biases and stereotypes. By questioning and dismantling societal norms that limit women's roles, we create an environment where their talents and potential can flourish. This involves promoting policies that address gender inequality, creating safe spaces free from harassment and violence, and actively challenging harmful attitudes and behaviors.

Institutional changes are important too. Companies and organizations should strive for gender parity in leadership positions, recognizing the value of diverse perspectives in decision-making. Political representation also matters as women's voices in governance and policymaking lead to more comprehensive and inclusive policies.

When we value and respect women, we unlock the incredible potential of half the population. We create a world that is fairer, more inclusive, and bursting with creativity. It's a collective effort that requires changing mindsets, challenging norms, and promoting equality. The rewards are immense as we build a brighter future for everyone, especially for young girls looking for themselves in the women they see. Young girls need strong role models they can look up to. As adult women reach their full potential, younger girls will be inspired to do the same.

It is crucial to challenge the status quo, dismantle oppressive systems, and amplify the voices of women. By doing so, we can create an environment where every girl and woman can thrive, where their dreams are nurtured, and where their worth is celebrated. And if there was one message I could share with every girl in the world, it is that *you matter*. No matter what culture you've been brought up in, how you've been treated, or what people think of you, your worth is deep, and there is a beautiful life of your design waiting for you.

Value Gives Power

The game of chess taught me a valuable lesson about life. It showed me that if I wanted to have power, I had to show my value. It was even more challenging for me in the culture I grew up in because women had little decision power and weren't highly valued in the same way that men were. As I grew older, I understood that I had to bring value to everything I did to gain power. I realized that power alone doesn't make you valuable. Honestly, you can be powerful and still be a terrible person. But value does give you power.

Just like the queen on the chessboard, who holds power because of her value, girls and young women have untapped power because of their worth. In chess, the queen has the highest value (nine), while the king doesn't have a specific point value. This made it clear to me that true power comes from recognizing and embracing your own value rather than seeking validation from others or conforming to societal ideas of worthiness.

This is a lesson we can share with all the incredible women and girls in our lives. It's not about being the most popular, the smartest, or the most athletic. It's about discovering the things inside you that give you value. Your kindness and character will guide you and serve you well on your journey. Embrace your unique strengths and qualities, and know that they hold tremendous power. By embracing your true value, you'll find the strength to overcome obstacles and make a positive impact in the world.

Empowering Our Queens

I was raised by my grandmother, mother, and aunt. They were superheroes in their own ways. Each of them had a different superpower that I hoped would pass down to me. But as I got older, I quickly realized that the strength they had was different from the kind I felt I needed to navigate the world. I didn't have many trailblazing women to look up to. My mother, while undoubtedly strong in her own way, did not possess the kind of power and influence that I longed to see in a role model inside our home. She was resilient, hardworking, and loving, but her cultural limitations prevented her from achieving the level of empowerment I desired. This lack of additional powerful female figures in my life made me keenly aware of the importance of providing young women and girls with strong role models who embody both strength and power.

Despite her own struggles, my mother demonstrated an incredible capability to navigate difficult circumstances and provide for our family. She had a successful career outside the home in the medical field and earned a lot of respect from her colleagues. The respect was different outside the home. Her value carried more weight in the hospital than in the house. She worked tirelessly to ensure our well-being and instilled in me a sense of determination and resilience. Her strength was evident in her dedication to her responsibilities and her balance of handling the cultural expectations placed on her inside the home. However, I yearned to see women who possessed not only personal strength but also the power to create change and inspire others.

Recognizing this gap in my own upbringing, I am committed to ensuring that the next generation of girls does not face the same lack of powerful role models. And if you look around in 2024, there is an abundance of strong, powerful women to look up to. We have to provide our daughters, athletes, and students with a diverse range of women who have achieved significant accomplishments and can serve as beacons of empowerment.

In celebrating the achievements of women from various fields, we can showcase a multitude of strong and powerful role models. These women can range from successful business leaders and accomplished professionals to influential artists, scientists, and activists. Their stories and achievements can inspire girls to dream big, break barriers, and realize their own potential.

Encouraging leadership among girls is another crucial aspect. Give them classes, small groups, and chances to develop their leadership skills, make decisions, and take initiative. In doing so, we empower them to become powerful agents of change in their communities and beyond. Through mentorship programs and connections with experienced women, we can provide guidance and support that nurtures their growth and helps them navigate the challenges they may face in their pursuit of power and influence.

Emphasizing self-worth is vital in this process. This self-assuredness becomes an essential foundation upon which they can build their personal power and make a difference in the world.

Creating safe and inclusive spaces is also important. Young women should feel free to express themselves, share their ideas, and explore their interests. These spaces should be characterized by respect, support, and the validation of their voices and perspectives. It can be as simple as asking intentional questions of your daughter on the way to school or having small group check-ins with your athletes. Ask them the difficult questions and be prepared to listen to their responses. Then, always ask how you can support them. You may not be the right person to give advice, but you can find someone who is.

And—hear me loud and clear—it is important to celebrate the achievements of girls, *no matter how big or small.* By acknowledging their hard work and celebrating and recognizing their successes, we reinforce their confidence, inspire them to continue striving, and showcase the power they possess to make positive impacts in their own lives and the lives of others.

In nurturing the potential of girls and young women, we bridge the gap that I personally experienced growing up. Let's pave the way for a future where girls can look up to a multitude of inspiring figures who demonstrate the true potential of female empowerment.

Think about It

1. Who were the strong and powerful women you looked up to while growing up, and how did they inspire you?

2. In what ways can we ensure that girls and young women have access to diverse role models from various fields and backgrounds?

3. What are some practical steps we can take to empower girls and young women to develop their leadership skills and make a positive impact in their communities?

Be about It

Seek out and celebrate diverse female role models: Take proactive steps to discover and showcase a wide range of strong and powerful women from various fields and backgrounds who can serve as role models for girls and young women. Research and share their stories, achievements, and contributions to inspire and empower girls and young women. Celebrate their accomplishments, both big and small, to reinforce the message that girls and young women can thrive and excel in any endeavor.

Foster mentorship and support networks: Encourage the establishment of mentorship programs and connections between experienced women and girls and young women. If you are in a position to mentor, offer guidance and support to girls and young women who can benefit from your experiences and insights. If you are a girl or young woman seeking guidance, actively seek out mentors who can provide valuable advice, encouragement, and support on your journey toward empowerment.

Create inclusive and empowering spaces: Take steps to create environments where girls and young women feel safe, respected, and valued. Foster inclusivity by actively listening to their voices, encouraging their participation, and validating their ideas and perspectives. Advocate for policies and initiatives that promote gender equity and provide equal opportunities for girls and young women to express themselves, develop their skills, and pursue their passions.

She did not stand alone,

but what stood behind

her, the most potent

moral force in her life,

was the love of her

father.

—HARPER LEE

CHAPTER 4

The GIRLdad Role

MY MOTHER CRIED the day I was born because I was not a boy. I grew up in a culture where I knew girls were not deeply wanted. In American culture, you may hear, "Congratulations! It's a girl!" But in Punjabi culture, it sounds more like, "I'm sorry. It's a girl. Maybe next time…" I entered the world in a state of apologies. Birthing a girl wasn't about dolls, pink dresses, and painted nails. It was more about responsibilities and dowries.

Sadly, my relationship with my father mirrored this cultural prejudice. Throughout my childhood, I deeply wanted his presence, his guidance, and his love, but it seemed that he was physically present without being truly there. But every Indian family I knew had the same level of absence from their father, so I accepted the cultural limitation and didn't really question it. I acknowledged that my father would be more involved in my brother's life and I would have different expectations placed on me. Later in life, I learned what I had been missing.

It was during my coaching career that I began to witness the power of deeply invested fathers in their daughters' lives. Observing the relationships between these fathers and their daughters, I saw firsthand how their investment and involvement had a profound impact on the young women I coached. The stark contrast in confidence levels between these young women and those who lacked a strong father figure was undeniable. It became clear to me that while the mother/daughter relationship is often emphasized, the relationship between fathers and daughters holds even greater significance.

I understand that not all fathers have the opportunity to live with their daughters because of various circumstances. Some may travel for work, others may be divorced, and there are even single fathers who face unique challenges. However, regardless of the living arrangement, the reality remains unchanged—the relationship between a father and his daughter fundamentally shapes the trajectory of her life and her future relationships. It is the most important relationship, the cross-gender bond that plays a pivotal role in her self-perception, her understanding of healthy relationships, and her interactions with men throughout her life.

Having a secure and nurturing relationship with her father is *absolutely* crucial for a young girl's development.

It impacts how she perceives herself, her worth, and her capabilities. It sets the standard for how she believes she should be treated by others, especially men, whether it be a partner, friend, coach, mentor, or teacher. The father/daughter relationship becomes the cornerstone upon which she builds her own self-esteem, confidence, and resilience. Dr. Nielsen's research at Wake Forest University concluded that when the father/daughter relationship is strong, women perform better in the "3Ms: Money, Men, and Mental Health."[17] It sounds a bit weird to say, but what it means is that when it comes to money, women who have strong relationships with their fathers tend to get better grades, graduate at higher rates, and are more likely to enter the STEM professions. For the second M, men, when women have a strong relationship with their fathers, they are more secure in themselves and less likely to need excessive attention from men. And finally, the third M: mental health. Women who have supportive relationships with their fathers tend to be more emotionally resilient and self-confident. So clearly, the father's role has a massive impact on the growth, development, and overall well-being of daughters.

Father Hunger

When girls lack a father figure in their lives, it often leads to what society commonly labels as "daddy issues" (though personally, I hate that term) or what research refers to as "father hunger." The consequences of this absence are significant and far-reaching. Girls who grow up without a strong father figure are more likely to engage in early sexual activity, experience emotional and behavioral challenges, and face an increased risk of becoming victims of domestic abuse in the future.[18] Additionally, they may be more susceptible to involvement in criminal activities, and the likelihood of living in poverty is higher (since often, they are in single-parent families).

These outcomes do not mean that girls without a strong father figure are doomed to predetermined lives. However, it does mean that they face additional obstacles and hardships. Imagine a young girl embarking on a journey, with her goals and aspirations represented by the road she travels. Along this road, she encounters numerous roadblocks and obstacles that are already present due to societal expectations and personal pressures. These roadblocks can include gender biases, cultural norms, limited opportunities, and other challenges that girls often face.

Having a father figure actively invested in her life is like having a full tank of gas for her journey. The father's involvement provides her with emotional support, guidance, and encouragement, acting as fuel to propel her forward. He helps her navigate these roadblocks, providing reassurance, advice, and a sense of security. With a full tank of gas, she has the confidence and resilience to overcome the challenges that come her way.

On the other hand, when a girl lacks a strong father figure, it's like attempting to navigate these roadblocks on an empty tank of gas. Without the support and guidance of a father figure, she may feel emotionally depleted and lacking the resources needed to face the challenges before her. It becomes much more difficult for her to overcome the roadblocks and continue on her journey. She may struggle with self-doubt, uncertainty, and a sense of emptiness, making it harder to persevere through the obstacles that arise.

In her book *Father Hunger: Fathers, Daughters, and the Pursuit of Thinness,* Dr. Margo Maine comments that "there is no substitute for a father's love...women who report having a close relationship with their father during childhood developed a strong sense of personal identity and positive self-esteem, as well as enjoying greater confidence in their adult relationships with men."[19]

The correlation between young women who have strong relationships with their fathers and strong senses of self-identity or confidence is evidenced all around us.

In my role as a coach for young women, I have seen the resilience in women who had strong relationships with their fathers. The women I have coached who had their fathers constantly assuring them of their abilities are more resilient when outcomes were not what they wanted. Fathers who are heavily attached to outcomes became a source of external pressures where fear of failure was heightened. Fathers who unknowingly or knowingly tied their daughters' self-worth to their performances created women who also tied their self-worth to their accolades. So, as we said in chapter 2, instead of praising the *outcome*, focus on praising the *effort*.

For me personally, this "father hunger" manifested as an intense desire to please and prove my worthiness. I was conditioned to believe that if I achieved good grades and performed well in various aspects of my life, I would finally gain my father's attention and approval. To this day, this battle continues within me. What saddens me is that my story is not unique; there are countless other girls who have faced similar struggles. Growing up, I witnessed other girls who shared my background and appearance experiencing the same challenges. These experiences profoundly impacted my self-confidence. Although I did not exhibit rebellion in the conventional sense until a much later age, I yearned to be perfect in an effort to compensate for the love and validation I lacked. As I grew older, I became increasingly rebellious in questioning societal expectations. This small amount of rebellion increased each time I was told what "Indian girls" were not allowed to do. The constraints felt so restricting that I left my family at eighteen, only to realize that even though I mustered enough courage and bravery to walk out, I lacked the self-confidence to navigate a world where acceptance came at a price. I found myself gravitating toward people who provided acceptance and leaned into relationships that weren't always healthy. I entered adulthood not really knowing what I was lacking but also unaware of what I needed.

The effects of father hunger are not isolated incidents but rather pervasive issues that affect numerous girls within various cultural contexts. No matter the racial demographic, political affiliation, religious background, or socioeconomic status, daughters crave a relationship with their fathers. The yearning for a strong father/daughter relationship is a universal longing that transcends boundaries. Every girl deserves the love, guidance, and support of a caring father figure, regardless of her cultural background. The absence of this relationship can have a profound impact on her sense of self-worth, confidence, and ability to navigate the complexities of life.

Physical versus Emotional Presence

Growing up, my father was in the home (physically present), but I never felt his investment in me (emotionally present). And although so much of that was based on tradition and gender roles in Punjabi families, I can honestly say I missed out. We didn't have conversations about my day and how school was going; we didn't have conversations about life or running or my thoughts. We didn't really have conversations at all. For me, getting good grades was the only way to be acknowledged. And

I strived for perfection in my academics because I so deeply desired to earn his attention.

I graduated from eighth grade with a 4.0—what I thought was perfection. I thought he would be happy and proudly beaming about this accomplishment. I dressed up for the graduation, and my aunt curled my hair so I could wear it down. My dad disapproved of his daughters wearing their hair down, and as a result, he would not stand next to me in any of the pictures. Instead of pride and affection, I received the silent treatment. It was my first feeling of being a disappointment.

There was no relationship and no security. To this day, this lack of relationship is so deeply rooted in my psyche. He was there, and I was there, and there was a chasm between us. And truthfully, that chasm was never bridged. I never heard "I love you" or "I support you" or "I'll be there" from my dad. I never heard "Keep trying. You'll get it next time" or "You've got this."

And the sad reality is that even in American culture, this disconnect between physical and emotional presence is all too common. It is a pattern that's easy to fall into, highlighting the challenges faced by fathers in balancing their work responsibilities with their roles as parents. But simply being physically present is not enough to cultivate a strong and meaningful bond with your daughter.

As a father, it is essential to go beyond the confines of societal expectations and actively invest in your relationship with your daughter (and your son as well, but that's a different book). While the demands of work can be overwhelming, you have to set aside time and energy to engage with your daughter on an emotional level. This means setting aside moments to have genuine conversations; listening attentively to their thoughts, feelings, and experiences; and providing the love, support, and guidance they need.

Give her attention not because she achieved something or did something well but simply because she is your daughter. Show her that you enjoy spending time with her even when it is not surrounding big events or some kind of scheduled activity. Emotional investment in your daughter's life involves more than just being physically present. It means actively participating in her life and taking an interest in her passions, dreams, and concerns. It means celebrating her achievements, offering words of encouragement, and providing a shoulder to lean on during challenging times. By doing so, you can instill in her a sense of security, self-worth, and confidence that will shape her future endeavors.

Breaking free from the stereotypes and expectations that surround fatherhood in some cultures is not an easy task. It requires a conscious effort to challenge societal norms and actively redefine the role of a father. By embracing emotional presence alongside physical presence, you have the power to shape a different reality—one that celebrates and encourages strong, loving, and meaningful relationships between fathers and daughters.

The Impact of a GIRLdad

You have probably heard that observation is the best teacher. And this is especially true when it comes to your relationship with your daughter. They are always observing: observing the way you interact with family members, them, and the world around you. This observation is quite literally training them on what to expect in future relationships. If we think of this on a very basic level, the way you treat your daughter will set a standard for how she should be treated in the future (by a partner, a friend, a coach, a mentor, a teacher, etc.). If you set a low bar, they will likely expect a low bar. If the person closest to them in the world treats them poorly—guess what—they will believe that it is okay to be treated that way. On an extreme measure, girls who grow up with abusive fathers are at a higher risk of experiencing abusive relationships in the future.[20] It is the role of the GIRLdad to show them how they should be treated and set that standard high. Not only are they observing what they will expect, but they are also observing how to interact in their own relationships. It's the typical thought process of, *Well, my dad does this, so that means it's okay.*

Having a strong, secure, trust-based relationship with your daughter is not going to eliminate the normal challenges that girls are going to experience with self-confidence, self-worth, and body image. Those are normal growing pains that come with being a girl.

But your relationship with her makes her more resilient. Having a constant, dependable relationship with her father doesn't make it less hard, but it makes your daughter tougher as she navigates challenges. She knows she has someone in her corner who is not going anywhere.

Aside from being a basketball legend, Kobe Bryant was known for being a girl dad. He doted on his daughters and often told people in interviews and in passing how much he loved having daughters. He famously commented in an interview, "I would have five more daughters if I could. I'm a girl dad."[21] This sparked the viral #GirlDad movement, with thousands of fathers posting pictures with their daughters and commenting about their special role. The movement reminded everyone that even in a society that traditionally values having sons, having a daughter is a unique and incredible privilege.

Filling the Gap

GIRLdads, you have the most important role in the world. As a father, your impact on your daughter's life is immeasurable. It is within your power to bridge the gap between physical and emotional presence, and in doing so, you can shape her journey in profound ways.

In my career coaching young women, I have witnessed dozens of relationships between fathers and daughters.

Some have been inspiring and empowering, while others have been devastating. The most heartwarming relationship I have observed was between an athlete named Sara and her dad. When Sara was just fourteen years old, her mother tragically passed away. Despite this loss, Sara excelled at running, catching my eye as a rising recruit. In the beginning, Sara struggled with self-worth, commitment, attachment, and a sense of belonging. Throughout this challenging period, Sara's dad demonstrated support by encouraging conversations filled with belief, he drove long distances and even slept in his truck to be present and cheer her on.

By the time she left the program five years later, Sara had grown into a confident and self-assured woman. It was not just the program that contributed to her growth, but the constant love and encouragement from her dad. He believed in her when she doubted herself, consistently showing up and providing care and support. Whether she was struggling at the back of the race or competing for victory, he cheered just as loudly. His conversations of concern with me were always about ensuring Sara's success, never placing blame or discouraging words. His impact made a significant impact on Sara's journey.

Our world needs more dads like Sara's dad. Recognize that your daughter yearns for your love, acceptance, and guidance. She seeks a connection with you that transcends superficial interactions. Your presence, both physical and emotional, holds the key to unlocking her potential and nurturing her self-esteem. By actively investing in her life, you can provide a solid foundation for her to grow, learn, and thrive.

It starts with making intentional choices. Take the time to truly see and understand your daughter. Engage in conversations that go beyond the surface level. Ask her about her dreams, her fears, and her aspirations. Show genuine interest in her hobbies, her passions, and her achievements. Celebrate her successes and offer a listening ear during her challenges. Let her know that you are her support, her rock, and her confidant.

This will look different when she is seven years old than when she is seventeen years old. As Meg Meeker points out in *Strong Fathers, Strong Daughters,* for your young daughter, it is enough for her to hear you say, "I love you." But your teenage daughter wants to know *why*.[22] What is it about her that makes you love her? Are you being sincere in what you say, or are you just telling her that you love her because you know you are supposed to say that? Praise her internal qualities before you praise her external beauty. Yes, you can always say that she looks beautiful on prom night or that her new haircut is super cute. But focus on the internal, on the things that matter. Compliment her for being generous, thoughtful, or hardworking.

What you compliment about your daughter will become what she frames as important. So, if you always focus on her beauty, she will frame beauty as important.

If you compliment academic achievements or athletics, that is what she will frame as important and will strive to excel in.

Embrace vulnerability in your relationship. Share your own experiences, triumphs, and failures. Let her witness your emotional depth and resilience. Teach her that it's okay to express her emotions, to be authentic, and to learn from setbacks. Your openness will foster a sense of trust and create an environment where she feels safe to explore her own identity and navigate the complexities of life. Make sure that she knows that you value her work and effort that result in various accomplishments, but *you love her* regardless of the accomplishments. Reinforce that her value is not tied to her achievements or success.

Break free from the confines of traditional gender roles. Challenge the notion that fathers should be distant providers and mothers the sole nurturers. Embrace the power of partnership with your co-parent. And regardless of your personal relationship, treat her mother with respect. You are literally setting the standard for how your daughter will expect to be treated in the future. Share the responsibilities of parenting, household chores, and decision-making. Let your daughter witness a model of equality and respect that will shape her expectations of future relationships.

Remember that being a GIRLdad is not about being perfect; it is about showing up consistently with love, empathy, and understanding. Be present for the small moments—the bedtime stories, the shared laughter, the ice cream trips, the whispered secrets. Cherish the milestones—the first steps, the school performances, the graduations. Your presence in these moments will create memories that will last a lifetime and will shape the woman your daughter becomes. Just be actively present.

GIRLdads, you have the unique opportunity to redefine fatherhood and to fill the gap between physical and emotional presence. Your investment in your daughter's life will have a ripple effect, extending far beyond the boundaries of your immediate family. It will contribute to a society where daughters are empowered, confident, and valued for who they are.

Think about It

1. In what ways can fathers strike a balance between their work responsibilities and their roles as emotionally invested parents? How can they create meaningful connections with their children despite the demands of modern life?

2. How can societal expectations and stereotypes surrounding fatherhood hinder the development of emotional bonds between fathers and their daughters? What steps can be taken to challenge and redefine these expectations?

3. Consider the impact of gender roles within your own family or community. How do these roles affect the emotional presence of fathers in their daughters' lives, and what can be done to promote equality and shared responsibility in parenting?

Be about It

Take intentional time to connect with your daughter: Dedicate regular, uninterrupted moments to connect with your daughter on an emotional level. Set aside at least ten minutes each day to have a meaningful conversation with her about her day, her thoughts, and her feelings. Show genuine interest and actively listen to create a safe space for her to express herself.

Prioritize quality time over quantity: Make a conscious effort to prioritize quality time with your daughter over the demands of work and other responsibilities. Plan activities or outings that allow for bonding and create opportunities for shared experiences. Whether it's a hike, cooking together, or simply enjoying a movie night, these moments foster emotional connections and strengthen your relationship.

Challenge traditional gender roles and expectations: Be proactive in challenging traditional gender roles and expectations that may hinder emotional bonds with your daughter. Take an active role in her emotional well-being by openly discussing emotions, encouraging vulnerability, and embracing your own emotional expression. Show her that being emotionally present and involved is a strength, breaking free from societal stereotypes.

Her soul is fierce.

Her heart is brave.

Her mind is strong.

—R.H. SIN

CHAPTER 5

Embracing the Power of Belief

DURING THE FIRST few years of my coaching career, I attended a leadership conference. The keynote speaker closed the conference with guidance that I will never forget. She said that the five most powerful words you can say to someone are "How can I help you?" The four most powerful words are "I believe in you." The three most powerful words are "I need you." The two most powerful words are "Thank you." And the most powerful word is "Yes."

I left that conference with the phrase "I believe in you" stuck in my brain. As a leader entrusted with the responsibility of coaching talented young athletes, I realized that belief is the singularly most potent gift I can offer them.

The Transformative Impact of Belief

Throughout my coaching career, those four words, "I believe in you," have been the cornerstone of my approach. They have shaped the very essence of my coaching philosophy and have been the catalyst for incredible transformations I have witnessed time and time again.

But it doesn't end with mere words. It goes far beyond that. I don't simply tell my athletes that I believe in them; I wholeheartedly believe in my belief in them. For me, belief is not just a sentiment; it is a form of investment. I am fully and completely invested in the goals and journeys of my athletes. It is a commitment that runs deep, an extreme dedication to their growth and success. When that belief is coupled with women who are obsessed with their craft in a healthy way, whose work ethic is on point, and who are committed to their own process and journey, magic can happen.

This investment of belief has a profound impact. It empowers my athletes to step outside their comfort zones, push their boundaries, and embrace challenges without the paralyzing fear of failure. When someone genuinely believes in you and you can feel it and know it through their deep investment, it becomes a wellspring of confidence—a confidence that emboldens them to take risks and pursue their dreams with determination.

Belief becomes the driving force that propels them forward, even in the face of adversity. It instills within them a sense of resilience, enabling them to bounce back from setbacks and to grow from experience. This belief becomes the bedrock upon which they build their own self-belief, their own conviction in their capabilities.

When they feel that belief and know that someone is fully invested in their success, it brings their courage to life. It fuels their motivation, their drive, and their determination. It gives them the strength to push through obstacles, to persevere when the going gets tough, and to unlock their true potential.

I have witnessed the transformational power of belief in action. I have seen athletes rise to incredible heights, achieving feats they once thought were beyond their reach. And in those moments, I am reminded of the profound impact that belief can have—the power it holds to unlock the endless possibilities that lie within each and every one of us.

So, I continue to build my coaching career around those four words—I believe in you. I continue to invest my belief in the aspirations and dreams of my athletes. And I am honored to witness the extraordinary journeys they undertake, knowing that belief is the driving force behind their success. The reality is that belief is not only impactful in the world of athletics but also in every part of a girl's or young woman's life. It includes academics, dreams, goals, aspirations, or truly anything they set their mind to. When they know someone believes in them, they can achieve just about anything.

The Power Is in the Words

The power of belief lies not only in the words we speak but also in how we express and share that belief with others. The way we demonstrate our belief may vary depending on the role we have in someone's life. As a coach, the way I convey my belief in my athletes, particularly in the case of young women, may differ from how a parent expresses belief in his or her child. However, regardless of the specific approach, one thing remains constant: Belief must be communicated and felt in order to have a meaningful impact.

Belief, in its essence, is a potent force. Yet, if it remains hidden and unexpressed, its power remains untapped and ineffective. It is not enough to silently hold belief within ourselves. If we fail to share that belief with others, they will not be aware of it or feel its influence. Belief, to be truly impactful, must be made visible and actively communicated.

Imagine a scenario where someone accomplishes a significant goal, and only afterward do we say, "I believed in you the whole time!" While the sentiment may be genuine, if we do not actively share our belief during the process, its impact is diminished. What truly matters is the belief we express throughout the journey—the support and encouragement we offer every step of the way.

When we say, "I believe in you," it has a profound effect on the mind of a young girl. It goes beyond mere words; it instills within her a deep understanding that she is not alone in her aspirations. It plants a seed of confidence that she can indeed achieve her dreams. Each step she takes becomes infused with purpose and meaning, knowing that it brings her closer to her ultimate goal.

It is my responsibility to actively demonstrate my belief in my athletes. I work hard to create an environment where they feel supported, valued, and empowered. I provide constructive feedback, guidance, and encouragement, ensuring that they know I genuinely believe in their potential. Through my actions and words, I cultivate a culture of belief—one that permeates their minds and fuels their determination. And believing in someone is not just a cheerleading position. It is holding someone to high expectations, reminding them of the dreams that they have, and pushing them to do and be their best. It's a deep accountability. I can't emphasize enough that belief without action is not transformative. Before every race, I write my young women a note card. That note card always ends with those four words—*I believe in you*. It's part of how I communicate my belief in them and am able to hold them accountable to their goals.

It is not enough to passively hold belief within ourselves. We must actively invest in those we believe in. We must be present, engaged, and committed to their growth.

By doing so, we become the catalysts for their success, igniting their inner fire and propelling them forward.

I strive to be an advocate for my athletes, consistently reinforcing my belief in their abilities. I create opportunities for them to showcase their skills, set attainable goals, face challenges, and learn from both victories and setbacks. Through this active engagement, I convey to them that their dreams are valid, attainable, and worthy of pursuit.

Belief, when actively expressed, has the power to transform lives. It instills a sense of confidence, resilience, and determination. It nurtures a growth mindset that embraces challenges as opportunities for growth. By actively saying, "I believe in you," we unlock the full potential within young girls and empower them to become the best versions of themselves.

Growth Mindset versus Fixed Mindset

I am passionate about empowering girls and young women to develop growth mindsets. It's not just about believing in their abilities; it's about equipping them with the mindset and tools to overcome challenges and achieve their full potential. Research has shown that mindset plays a crucial role in shaping their future successes and well-being. [23]

A growth mindset is the belief that intelligence, abilities, and talents can be developed through effort and perseverance. On the other hand, a fixed mindset is the belief that these qualities are predetermined and unchangeable. When girls and young women have fixed mindsets, they may become trapped in self-limiting beliefs, doubt their abilities, and avoid challenges for fear of failure.

The dangers of a fixed mindset can have a profound impact on the rest of their lives. Girls and young women with fixed mindsets may shy away from pursuing their passions and goals, believing that their abilities are fixed and they cannot improve. These mindsets can hinder their personal, academic, and career growth, limiting their opportunities for success and fulfillment.

Recent research has highlighted the importance of promoting a growth mindset in girls and young women. A study conducted by *The Journal of Youth and Adolescence* found that when girls were taught about the malleability of intelligence and the power of effort, they showed increased motivation and resilience in academic settings.[24] By nurturing a growth mindset, we can empower girls to embrace challenges, persist in the face of setbacks, and achieve higher levels of success.

Another study conducted by *Personality and Social Psychology Bulletin* in 2021 emphasized the impact of mindset on career aspirations among young women.

They found that those with a growth mindset were more likely to pursue challenging career paths (specifically STEM-related careers), set ambitious goals, and overcome gender stereotypes.[25] By cultivating a growth mindset, we can inspire girls and young women to break through societal barriers, pursue their passions, and strive for leadership roles in their chosen fields.

As leaders, we have to promote growth mindsets among girls and young women. With my program, I strive to create an environment that encourages them to embrace challenges, view failure as a stepping stone to success, and persist in the face of adversity. I provide constructive feedback that focuses on effort, progress, and the learning process, reinforcing the belief that abilities can be developed through dedication and hard work.

Belief Creates Self-Belief

Belief has a remarkable power to create self-belief in young women. As my athletes navigate the ups and downs, the challenges and triumphs of a season, my belief in them becomes a catalyst for their own belief in themselves. It is a profound transformation that occurs when external belief merges with internal conviction.

Consider this scenario: Imagine someone telling you, day after day, that you have the capability to achieve a specific goal. Over time, these words of encouragement and belief seep into your consciousness. You begin to challenge the doubts and insecurities that may have held you back. Gradually, you start to internalize this belief, and it becomes a part of your own self-perception.

This process of belief begetting belief is a powerful phenomenon. My role in the lives of young women goes beyond imparting tactical strategies and skills. I recognize the immense value in fostering a mindset of self-belief within each young woman I work with. By consistently affirming their abilities, by reminding them of their strengths, and by acknowledging their progress, I am actively contributing to the development of their self-belief.

I witness the transformation unfolding before my eyes. With every practice, every race, and every obstacle they overcome, my athletes begin to recognize their own resilience, determination, and potential. The belief I have in them acts as a mirror, reflecting back their own capabilities. It becomes a guiding light that illuminates the path toward their goals.

My ultimate aspiration is to empower these young women to believe in themselves. I want them to recognize their inherent worth and the endless possibilities that lie within their grasp. As they cultivate self-belief, they become the architects of their own success, unafraid to dream big and willing to pursue their passions with unapologetic commitment.

When women believe in themselves, they become unstoppable forces of change. They break through societal barriers, challenge stereotypes, and shatter glass ceilings. They inspire others with their resilience, determination, and dreams. By nurturing belief in themselves, we are fostering a generation of empowered women who will go on to make a profound impact in their communities, professions, and the world at large.

It is my mission as a coach to create an environment where self-belief can flourish. I foster a culture that celebrates individual strengths, encourages risk-taking, and supports personal growth. I do not always get it right, and you won't either, but if the actions match the intentions, it will make a difference. Through mentoring, constructive feedback, accountability, and creating opportunities for success, I empower my athletes to recognize their own potential and believe in their unique abilities.

Think about It

1. How has belief played a role in your own life? Reflect on a time when your belief in yourself or a specific dream helped you overcome challenges and achieve success.

2. Consider the impact of belief on the lives of the girls and young women you know. How can you actively foster a culture of belief and empowerment in their lives? What actions can you take to support and encourage their dreams?

3. Consider the power of collective belief and support. How can we come together as a community to uplift and empower young girls? Reflect on ways in which you can collaborate with others to create a network of encouragement and inspiration.

Be about It

Engage in open conversations about dreams and aspirations: Take the time to have meaningful conversations with your daughter about her dreams and aspirations. Ask her about her long-term goals and interests. Listen attentively and show genuine interest in her ideas. By actively engaging in these conversations, you can better understand her aspirations and provide the support she needs.

Offer practical support and guidance: Once you understand your daughter's dreams, proactively offer your support and guidance. Discuss potential steps or resources that can help her reach her goals. Encourage her to explore different opportunities, provide mentorship, or help her find relevant educational programs or extracurricular activities. By actively assisting her in her pursuit, you can foster belief and empowerment in her abilities.

Collaborate with others to create a supportive network: Reach out to other parents, mentors, or community members who share a similar goal of empowering young girls. Organize workshops, networking events, or mentorship programs that provide a supportive environment for girls to share their dreams and receive guidance. By collaborating with others, you can create a strong support network that uplifts and empowers girls to pursue their aspirations.

It is not joy that makes us grateful; it is gratitude that makes us joyful.

—DAVID STEINDL-RAST

CHAPTER 6

Cultivating Gratitude for Confidence

EVERY MORNING, ON my drive to work, I take a moment to verbalize the things I'm grateful for. It's a simple act, but it has a profound impact on how I navigate through the day. You see, it's not just about appreciating what I have: my health, my family, my team, and the blessings in my life. It's about the way gratitude shapes my mindset and boosts my self-confidence.

From my personal experience, there's a clear connection between gratitude, happiness, and self-assurance. When I approach life with a gratitude lens and an abundance mentality, something magical happens—my confidence and belief in myself grow stronger.

It's not about having all the answers. It's about finding what works for you and embracing it. For me, starting the day with gratitude sets the stage for a positive outlook. It's like putting on a pair of confidence-boosting glasses that help me see the world in a brighter light. Research shows that not only is gratitude a valued trait but also gratitude creates a sense of abundance and increases happiness.[26] Honestly, it's not that surprising—you've probably heard the phrase "grateful people are happy people," and it rings true.

And it hasn't just worked for me—I've watched it change the perspectives and confidence of the young women I coach.

Gratitude and Confidence versus Entitlement

Gratitude and entitlement can't coexist. You might have noticed entitlement creeping into the attitudes of young people nowadays, but the truth is it has always existed. Maybe we just didn't pay much attention to it when it was within ourselves or didn't recognize it. Entitlement is all about expecting things to happen to you and for you without putting in the work. It's like skipping the effort and just assuming things will come your way.

Gratitude, on the other hand, sits in direct contrast with entitlement. Gratitude brings a sense of peace and contentment. When you express gratitude, you're rewiring your mindset—literally. Because of neuroplasticity, the brain is able to create new neural connections. So, if someone is living in a negative, ungrateful mindset, his or her thinking will be skewed negatively. But if someone wants to change this negative pattern, his or her brain can create these new, positive pathways to restructure that person's thinking and mindset.[27] It's about recognizing that you can overcome challenges and stay committed to your goals. The act of expressing gratitude creates a positive mindset that boosts your confidence, both in the work you put in and in your ability to chase your dreams.

Gratitude and confidence are closely related. Gratitude creates a positive energy, and that energy in turn creates confidence. When you're truly grateful for everything you have, you start to realize the abundance in your life. And that realization gives you a sense of confidence. It's like acknowledging all the good things around you empowers you to believe in yourself and your abilities.

As a coach in today's landscape, it's easy to see why athletes struggle with entitlement. I constantly remind them of our team culture, which is faith, trust, and love, all built on gratitude. It really does make a difference. Every year, freshmen join us, and they're usually overwhelmed with gratitude for all the Nike gear and opportunities our program provides. But as time goes on, a sense of comfort sets in, and gratitude lessens as the standard expectation of how we operate becomes the norm. Once it becomes an expectation, a small amount of entitlement sneaks in.

The problem with entitlement is that it's not just about expecting things; it's also about expecting specific outcomes. And that mindset bypasses the necessary work. By focusing solely on the end result, you're robbing yourself of the growth and opportunities that come from the process. Similarly, confidence isn't built solely on the outcome of doing hard things; it's built in the process itself. It's about embracing the challenges and pushing through them, knowing that growth happens along the way.

It all comes down to a shift in perspective. As a team, we have to approach everything through the lens of gratitude. By cultivating gratitude, we remind ourselves of the value in the journey, appreciate what we have, and find the confidence to tackle any obstacles that come our way.

The Boomerang Effect

When I see women on my team struggling with confidence, I've found a simple assignment that works wonders. I ask them to take a moment and look around at their teammates. Who else might be facing their own confidence challenges? Once they've identified someone, I encourage them to focus on uplifting that person for the next week. It could be writing thoughtful notes, sending text messages, offering words of encouragement during practices, or simply showing them love and support.

And you know what? It usually has an amazing result. The runner who initially lacked confidence finds herself in a much better place mentally. She becomes more self-assured, builds stronger relationships with her teammates, and develops a deeper sense of empathy. It's like a positive chain reaction. When we build people up who are going through the same grueling practices or college life alongside us, that building up comes back to us like a boomerang in the form of increased confidence. And it comes back to gratitude. The link between confidence and gratitude is fascinating to me—gratitude truly increases confidence. And when we're focusing on others, it makes us more grateful for what we have and, in turn, increases our confidence.[28]

We're often wired to focus on what we lack. Whether it's scrolling through social media, comparing ourselves to a friend, or feeling the pressure of competition, our minds naturally gravitate toward what others have that we don't. But when we take a step back and appreciate the people around us, especially those going through similar challenges, something magical happens. That building boomerangs back to us, filling us with confidence and reminding us of our own strengths.

Practicing Gratitude

Incorporating gratitude into your life, as well as the lives of the girls and young women you support, can have a profound impact on overall well-being and happiness. There are numerous simple and effective ways to infuse gratitude into daily routines.

One approach that has proven helpful with my team is the use of a morning gratitude check-in. We have an app, Status Strong, where, each day, team members identify their levels of gratitude using colors like red, yellow, or green. This practice creates a moment of reflection and encourages individuals to pause and think about what they are grateful for. It sets a positive tone for the day ahead and helps cultivate a mindset of appreciation.

Another powerful method is keeping a gratitude journal. Taking a few moments at the end of each day to jot down things you are grateful for can have a significant impact. It could be as simple as acknowledging small moments of joy, acts of kindness from others, or personal achievements. By writing them down, you create a tangible record of positivity and a reminder of the good in your life.

Sharing gratitude with others is another meaningful practice. During conversations with your daughter or the young women you support, ask questions that prompt reflection, such as, "What are you grateful for?" or "What are you most excited about for today?" These inquiries not only open up dialogue but also encourage introspection and raise awareness of the positive aspects of life. By expressing gratitude together, you foster a sense of appreciation and create an uplifting atmosphere.

Embracing gratitude as a daily practice can transform perspectives and enhance well-being. By incorporating these simple but powerful habits into your routine, you create space for appreciation and positivity to flourish. It's a beautiful way to nurture gratitude within yourself and inspire those around you to adopt a similar mindset.

Remember: gratitude is not just a fleeting emotion. It is a mindset that can be cultivated through intentional practices. Establishing a culture of gratitude can lead to greater contentment, resilience, and overall happiness.

Think about It

1. Have you considered introducing gratitude practices to the girls and young women you support? How might it benefit their well-being?

2. How can expressing gratitude help boost the confidence of the girls and young women you invest in?

3. Have you noticed entitlement attitudes among the girls and young women you work with? How can gratitude help promote a stronger work ethic?

Be about It

Introduce a daily gratitude practice: Encourage the girls and young women you invest in to start their day by jotting down three things they are grateful for. This simple act of reflection can set a positive tone for their day and help cultivate a mindset of appreciation.

Foster gratitude discussions: During conversations and group sessions, incorporate questions that prompt reflection and gratitude sharing. Encourage the girls and young women to express what they are grateful for and what excites them about their day. This practice not only raises awareness of the positive aspects of their lives but also creates a supportive and uplifting atmosphere.

Lead by example: Embrace and embody gratitude in your own life. Share your personal experiences of how gratitude has positively impacted you. When girls and young women see you practicing and valuing gratitude, they are more likely to adopt and integrate it into their own lives. Be a role model and demonstrate the power of gratitude through your actions and words.

Just when the caterpillar thought the world was ending, she became a butterfly.

—CHUANG TZU

CHAPTER 7

Failing Better

IN 2023, MY cross country women's team at BYU was favored to be in the top three at the National Championship. We had won the Big 12 Cross Country Championships and were ranked third in the NCAA. They were by far one of my most talented teams. In the past, I had teams that earned podium finishes, with the 2021 team crowned as NCAA Champions. I knew this team had similar potential to those teams. We did the regular workouts, I believed in them, and I did my best to make sure that they were ready. I thought they were ready. But then, on race day, everything changed.

Nothing terrible happened before the race; no tragic or catastrophic event happened to any of the runners. But as they stepped up to the starting line, I started feeling less confident. Originally, I'd felt confident that we had the potential to win or at least place in the top four. But there was something off from the previous teams I had coached to top finishes. It wasn't physical preparation or talent, but I saw wavering bouts of confidence. About halfway through the race, I knew my gut was right. We ended up finishing fourteenth in the NCAA championship meet, barely hanging on when we should have been competing with the top teams in the country.

This was the first time in my career that my team had that kind of finish. The pressure of the meet turned into panic, and we could not overcome the emotions and expectations. There was a fear of failure that could not be overturned by faith. For me, it was the first time in my career that I felt like I'd entirely failed my team. I questioned myself, and I wasn't sure I could handle the aftermath of letting them down by inadequately preparing them for the emotional needs of this caliber of competition. It hit me really hard. But I picked up myself so that I could pick up my women. And in the wake of this awful, surprising failure, I posted the following caption on my Instagram page:

> Just when the caterpillar thought the world was ending, she became a butterfly. This isn't the caption I envisioned writing after the NCAA Championships. I made a promise this year to use my women's successes to inspire other young girls in the sport. So here it goes regardless: to all the girls/women who are struggling

> with a setback, who have failed, who have fallen short of their goal, who feel a little lost and disappointed, keep believing. This one hurts as the physical preparation was there. We will be back as stronger and tougher versions of ourselves. Grateful for these women and our support systems. Leading at 2k, 3rd at 4k, 5th at 5k, and fell to 14th for the finish. Not the race plan but no words for that kind of crumble. Disappointed in the ending but not in the season. **We will keep working hard until our butterfly moment.**

Looking back on it now, I became a better coach because of that moment. The world sort of felt like it was ending. I felt like I had let down not only my team but also a lot of girls and women who look to our program for inspiration.

Three months later, I took the same team of women to the NCAA Indoor Championships, and we had a dominant showing. We scored more points than any distance program in the country. Who we became through the process of failure made both me and the team more resilient and stronger than if we had been a podium team at Cross Country NCAA. What our women did was absolutely nothing short of incredible. They were the women who still tried. They were the women who bounced back. They were the women who failed better.

Framing Failure

Processing the failure at the NCAA Championship was crucial for me and my team. I recognized the importance of fully acknowledging and understanding what had happened in order to move forward. However, I found myself unsure of how to navigate this process since it was new territory for me. Personally, I felt a sense of shock. I was frustrated and disappointed with myself, blaming my lack of mental preparation.

Seeking reassurance, I turned to colleagues, only to receive responses like "Welcome to the club" or "You're lucky you haven't experienced it before, but it's part of the journey." Their seemingly dismissive attitude made me feel even worse. Some even chuckled and took delight in our finish. People questioned whether I would leave college coaching to focus on professional coaching, and I had no immediate answers. I knew I was the same coach who navigated the global pandemic with a "Win the Wait" attitude. We came back from it very strong, winning the NCAA Championship. I knew I had encountered many personal setbacks and come back stronger. The difference with this one was I knew I let my team down. I overlooked potential mental weaknesses and an unbalanced team chemistry. I wasn't sure I or we could come back better from it. But a conversation with my postcollegiate coach changed everything.

During our call, my coach, Frank Gagliano, posed a

simple yet powerful question: "What are you going to do about it?" That question reframed the failure in my mind and fueled my determination to learn from it, do better, and help my athletes move forward.

Initially, I encouraged the young women on my team to write about their experiences with failure. From a young age, we are taught to view failure negatively, creating an emotional connection that lingers throughout our lives. We are told to forget about it and move forward. We tend to avoid failure, tiptoeing around it, and girls, in particular, often fear failure more than anything else. Yet the reality is that many successful individuals credit their failures as stepping stones to success. Failure can be either debilitating or a hurdle on the path to growth. So, to me, it was very important that they write out their feelings and emotions about the race. I wanted them to heal from it by fully processing it. I had each of my young women write a letter about what she was feeling. I did the same. (Some of my feelings are written above.) This wasn't just a "move-on" race. It was a National Championship. A lot of people had a lot of things to say about it, and the team was on a public platform.

Failure is framed as something inherently bad. We tell students they "failed a paper" or "failed a class," implying that they didn't master something and cannot move forward. It becomes a definitive end. Even in competitive sports, when young girls lose a game, it is often seen as a failure. However, failure is not the end-all, be-all. It opens up infinite possibilities. When we think about failure and how we learn from it, we should view it as a comma, not a period. Failure carries emotions that impact self-worth and self-value. While we don't need to celebrate failure, we mustn't let the fear of failing deter us from trying.

The emotional connection to failure needs to dissipate. We should perceive failure as a hurdle on our journeys rather than the finish line. The emotional framework we develop around failure during our formative years profoundly impacts us throughout our lives. In her now famous speech at a Harvard commencement, J. K. Rowling said that failure in life is not only inevitable but also beneficial.[29] If we can reframe failure as something that is bound to happen and has its own value, we can empower young women to overcome their fears and create meaningful lives for themselves.

So, how can we make this shift in perception?

First, let's emphasize resilience. Encourage young women to develop resilience by recognizing that setbacks and failures are natural parts of life. Help them understand that resilience grows when we face challenges, learn from our mistakes, and keep going no matter what.

Next, let's *normalize* failure. Create an environment where failure is seen as a learning opportunity rather than something to be ashamed of. Share stories of successful individuals who have experienced failure and show how it ultimately led them to grow and achieve great things. By doing this, we challenge the idea that failure means we're not good enough.

Teaching a growth mindset is also important. Help young women understand that their abilities and intelligence can be developed through hard work and effort. Encourage them to embrace challenges, see mistakes as chances to improve, and believe in their own capacities to learn and grow from failures.

Building a support system is crucial too. Create networks of mentors, teachers, and peers who can provide guidance, encouragement, and advice. Let young women know that it's okay to ask for help and share their failures with others. Having a supportive environment can make all the difference in how they handle setbacks.

Finally, let's celebrate effort and progress. Instead of solely focusing on outcomes, let's recognize and appreciate the effort and progress young women make. By valuing their determination, resilience, and perseverance, we reinforce the idea that failure is not the end but a stepping stone toward personal and professional growth.

Failing Better, Failing Forward

As a team, we made a conscious decision to reframe our failure and embrace the concept of failing forward. We understood that failure is an inevitable part of the journey, and rather than being discouraged by it, we chose to fully process our setbacks and keep trying.

I've always been a fan of Michael Jordan, but I think people often miss the reality of failure as a catalyst for success. The reality is that it's not about the failure—it's about how you recover from it. He said, "I've missed more than nine thousand shots in my career. I've lost almost three hundred games. Twenty-six times, I've been trusted to take the game-winning shot and missed. I've failed over and over and over again in my life. And that is why I succeed."[30]

When our initial setback felt like the end of the world, I constantly reminded my young women of the potential of these butterfly moments. We understood that even in the darkest times, there was an opportunity for something remarkable to emerge. So, instead of avoiding failure or dwelling on it, we confronted it head-on.

We took the time to emotionally process our failure as a team. We openly discussed our feelings, analyzed our mistakes, and identified areas for improvement. By doing so, we were able to extract valuable lessons from our setbacks and turn them into motivation for the future.

Our sights were set on the Indoor NCAA Championship. We understood that failing better meant persistently trying again despite the fear of facing failure once more. We embraced the idea that success is not a linear path but the result of relentless effort and commitment.

This growth mindset is not limited to the sports arena; it applies to various aspects of life. We recognize that failure is an essential part of personal and professional growth. Many successful individuals and entrepreneurs have encountered failure along their journeys. They have learned to process their failures fully, extract valuable insights, and use them as stepping stones toward future achievements.

It is through this process of fully embracing failure, learning from it, and persistently trying again that we can unlock our true potential. Each attempt brings us closer to success, and each failure provides an opportunity for growth. By facing failure head-on and refusing to be discouraged, we become individuals who are not defined by setbacks but empowered by them.

So, we committed ourselves to the pursuit of excellence, knowing that failure was not the end but a stepping stone on the path to success. We understood that by fully processing failure, trying again and again with renewed determination, we would not only grow as individuals but also achieve remarkable things as a team.

Butterfly Moments

The NCAA Indoor Championship in the spring of 2024 is something I will never forget. Just three months after our devastating defeat, my team of young women lined up on the starting line and set out to make BYU history. Every single young woman who competed in the NCAA Cross Country Championship race qualified for the NCAA Indoor Championship. It was the most beautiful butterfly moment of my career. What had been a dark, world-ending feeling after the last championships had turned into something remarkable. After the races, someone asked me how we had done it and how I felt about it. And really, all I could say was that these women were believers, and I believed in them. In the midst of the struggle, in the midst of the pain, I believed in them, and they believed in themselves. And what a difference that makes.

A few weeks after the NCAA Indoor Championship, I found a surprise on my desk. My young women had framed a picture of the team. The gold frame was covered in butterflies. The card attached read: *Thank you for teaching us that failure is not final.* It made me a little teary-eyed thinking of all the girls and young women whose butterfly moments are just waiting to happen—waiting for someone to believe in them, to help them reframe failure, and to help them fail forward into greatness. Now, that world—a world full of butterfly moments for girls and young women—would be a truly beautiful world.

Think about It

1. How can you reframe failure as a catalyst for success to positively impact the mindset and approach of girls and young women?

2. Why is it important to create a safe space for girls and young women to fully process failure, openly discuss their feelings, and learn from their mistakes?

3. In what ways can failure be viewed as a stepping stone on the path to growth and personal development for the girls and young women you support?

Be about It

Reframe failure as a catalyst for success and personal growth: Encourage girls and young women to view failure as a stepping stone on the path to success. Help them understand that setbacks and mistakes are opportunities for learning and growth. Share stories of famous individuals who faced failures but persevered to achieve greatness. By reframing failure in a positive light, you can inspire them to embrace challenges, develop resilience, and persist in the face of adversity.

Create a safe space for processing failure and discussing emotions: Establish an environment where girls and young women feel safe to fully process failure, openly discuss their feelings, and learn from their mistakes. Encourage them to share their experiences, challenges, and setbacks without judgment. Foster a supportive atmosphere that emphasizes learning from failures rather than dwelling on them. By creating this safe space, you empower them to develop growth mindsets and build emotional resilience.

Promote the concept of failing forward and its broader application: Help girls and young women understand that failure is not a permanent state but a stepping stone toward growth and personal development. Encourage them to see failures as opportunities to learn, adjust their strategies, and continue progressing. Emphasize that failing forward applies not only to specific activities or sports but also to all areas of their lives, including academics, relationships, and personal goals. By embracing this concept, they can approach challenges with positive mindsets and persevere in the face of obstacles.

A girl should be two things: who and what she wants.

—COCO CHANEL

CHAPTER 8

Just Dream It

WHEN I WAS in fifth grade, something happened that changed my perspective on dreams. My teacher, Mrs. Sparks, gave us a questionnaire to get to know us better. One of the questions asked about our dreams. I had never really thought about it before, so I wrote down what my parents wanted for me: My parents wanted me to go to college and study medicine.

But then Mrs. Sparks did something unexpected. She called me over one day and showed me my paper. She explained that my dreams shouldn't be what other people want for me; they should be my own. She handed the paper back to me and said, "Your dream can be anything you want, something you're passionate about and love doing."

I was caught off guard and asked her, "Even for someone like me?" I was worried that being a Punjabi girl might limit my dreams.

But Mrs. Sparks replied, "Especially for someone like you."

Her words made me think differently. Up until then, I never even knew what a dream was. But Mrs. Sparks's words sparked something inside me. I started asking myself what I really wanted in life and how I could make it happen.

It wasn't an instant revelation. It took time to figure out what truly mattered to me. I had to let go of the need to please others and strive for perfection. It was a process of discovering my own passions and desires.

But with Mrs. Sparks's initial nudge in my heart, I began exploring and uncovering my dreams. I realized that I didn't have to limit myself to what others expected of me. I could dream big and pursue what made me happy.

It wasn't always easy. There were moments when I doubted myself and wondered if my dreams were valid. But that conversation with Mrs. Sparks stayed with me. She taught me that my dreams were important, regardless of my background or gender.

Today, I'm grateful for that conversation with Mrs. Sparks. It set me on a path of self-discovery and empowerment. It taught me that my dreams are worth pursuing and that I have the power to shape my own future.

The Power of a Dream

Fast-forward from my fourth-grade experience to my current career as a running coach, and one thing remains constant: the significance I place on dreams. Every season, without fail, I begin by asking the young women I work with about their dreams. I want to dive deep into their hearts and discover their deepest desires—the things they may be too afraid to share with anyone else. It's an invaluable opportunity for them to reflect on and identify what they truly want, whether it's in their athletic pursuits, social lives, academics, or aspirations for the future.

Over time, I have witnessed an undeniable truth: Girls with dreams become women with vision. It's awe-inspiring to observe how these young athletes carefully construct lifestyles that align with and support the pursuit of their dreams. I've seen their dreams evolve and transform, growing in size and taking unexpected turns along the way. Some women have achieved their deepest aspirations, while others have come just shy of reaching them. But regardless of the outcome, one thing remains clear: Dreams are not static; they are dynamic and ever-changing.

Dreams have a way of expanding our horizons, redirecting our paths, and pushing us to pivot when necessary. Yet the most crucial aspect is the ability to have a dream and to boldly articulate it. Because from that dream, a powerful goal emerges—a tangible target that propels us forward and serves as a roadmap for turning our aspirations into reality. I firmly believe that our dreams are intertwined with our purpose. When we live with purpose, we become intentional about the people we strive to become and the means by which we achieve our dreams.

Encouraging young women to identify and vocalize their dreams is of utmost importance to me. Whether as mentors, parents, teachers, or coaches, we must ensure that we are consistently asking this question of young girls. By doing so, we grant them permission to dream, and when they verbalize their dreams, they become accountable for setting goals and acting. This accountability provides a powerful framework for their growth and development.

To witness a young woman bravely declare her dream is a remarkable sight. It signifies a profound shift—a declaration of her worthiness, her ambitions, and her potential. It is our collective responsibility to create an environment where these dreams can flourish and young women are empowered to pursue their passions with determination and resilience.

So, ask the question. Ask about your daughter's dreams. It will ignite the spark of possibility in the hearts of young girls. Remind them that their dreams matter and that they have the power to shape their own futures. In creating a culture that values dreams and encourages goal-setting, we instill within them the confidence and strength to pursue their aspirations fearlessly.

Dreams versus Expectations

If my own story is any indication, it's all too common for young girls to live their lives according to the expectations of others. This is why doing the work to find out what they are passionate about is extremely important.

When I ask one of my young athletes about their dreams, I often get responses that relate to the sport. But as they spend time in the program, that dream expands from what they want to achieve to who it is they want to become.

It's a heartbreaking realization to witness a young woman grappling with the weight of external expectations. I've seen it in the furrowed brows and uncertain voices of those who struggle to separate their own dreams from the dreams thrust upon them. Society, family, and friends all play a role in shaping these expectations, sometimes unintentionally overshadowing the individual's own aspirations.

I understand the importance of creating a safe space for these young girls to explore their true dreams without being burdened or influenced by external pressures. It's about empowering them to break free from the shackles of expectation and discover their own passions, their own visions for the future.

True dreams are born from within, from the depths of our hearts and souls. They are not crafted to please others or meet preconceived notions of success. Dreams are personal, unique, and deeply intimate. They reflect who we are at our core and what truly resonates with us.

When a young girl can distinguish her own dreams from the expectations placed upon her, a remarkable transformation occurs. It's as if a weight is lifted off her shoulders and she can finally breathe in the freedom to embrace her authentic desires. She begins to dream without limitations, without fear of disappointing others. Her dreams become a reflection of her own voice, her own aspirations.

The Power of the Process

I repeat this phrase often: Girls with dreams become women with vision. When young girls are encouraged to articulate their dreams, map out the steps toward achieving them, and identify the support they need along the way, they are equipped with a clear process that empowers them to pursue anything they desire. It is not solely about the outcome or the grand vision; it is about the actions taken to reach those aspirations.

In our society, there is often an excessive emphasis on the end result. We celebrate the achievements and accolades of individuals like Caitlin Clark, the number one WNBA draft pick in 2024. But have we truly pondered what it took for her to reach that pinnacle? If we delve deep, we would likely discover that it required countless hours in the gym, saying no to social outings or movie nights in favor of honing her skills. It involved early mornings, late nights, and sacrifices that may not have always felt "fair." It was the relentless dedication and willingness to put in the work that transformed her into the icon she is today. Her habits, forged through the process, shaped her success—her dream alone was not enough.

Instead of solely celebrating the outcome, it is crucial for parents and mentors to praise the process itself. The truth is, far more is learned and gained through the journey than through the end result alone. Consider the analogy of "sweat equity." When you invest your hard-earned money in purchasing a car, you understand its value. You're more likely to take care of it, and you feel frustration when it is mistreated or damaged. Similarly, a dream that you have invested in and worked tirelessly for becomes all the more meaningful when it is realized. The hard work, dedication, and effort put into the process will not go unrewarded, even if the dream remains just slightly out of reach.

By shifting our focus to the process, we instill in young girls a profound understanding of the significance of their journeys. We teach them that progress, growth, and the lessons learned along the way are invaluable. We empower them to embrace the challenges, setbacks, and triumphs that shape their character and resilience. It is through the process that they cultivate the skills, mindset, and determination necessary to navigate the ever-changing landscape of their dreams.

One Step at a Time

I have the privilege of witnessing the transformative power of dreams firsthand. I've seen girls and young women surpass their own expectations, break through barriers, and achieve feats they once thought were beyond their reach. Dreams have the incredible ability to ignite passion, fuel determination, and unlock untapped potential. It is my mission to inspire and empower these young girls to dream big, and I implore parents and mentors to foster and nurture those dreams.

In the world of running, just as in life, the journey toward success is rooted in the process. It begins with a dream, a vision of what could be. When a young girl envisions herself crossing the finish line, whether it's a small race or an Olympic event, it sparks a fire within her. That flame of aspiration must be fanned, encouraged, and embraced.

Be the wind beneath their wings. Embrace their dreams with open hearts and let them know that their aspirations are valid and valuable. Encourage them to dream big, to set audacious goals, and to believe in their ability to achieve them. Establish an environment of support and belief to provide them with the foundation they need to soar.

But dreams alone are not enough. Encourage these young girls to set goals that are specific, measurable, and attainable. Help them understand that dreams are not distant fantasies; they are destinations waiting to be reached. By setting smaller goals along the way, they can celebrate victories, track progress, and feel the exhilaration of moving closer to their dreams.

As parents and mentors, you have the power to instill in these young girls the value of consistent effort and daily habits. Teach them that dreams are not achieved overnight but are the result of dedicated practice, perseverance, and a commitment to improvement. Help them establish routines that align with their dreams—whether it's a daily or weekly checklist, find rubrics where they can measure their progress. These habits will empower them to make strides every day and build the resilience necessary to overcome obstacles along the way.

In nurturing their dreams, remind these young girls that setbacks and challenges are not signs of failure but opportunities for growth. Celebrate their victories but also guide them through moments of disappointment. Teach them that resilience and determination are the cornerstones of success. Through the highs and lows, encourage them to keep pushing forward, to learn from each experience, and to embrace the journey with unwavering enthusiasm.

Create a supportive and empowering community that believes in the potential of every young girl. We should celebrate their dreams, guide them through the process, and inspire them to dream big. By fostering an environment where dreams are cherished and nurtured, we empower young girls to become the confident, resilient, and unstoppable individuals they are destined to be.

I urge you to be the catalysts of dreams. Embrace the power of encouragement, provide the guidance needed, and instill in these young girls the belief that their dreams are within their grasp.

Think about It

1. What are the dreams and aspirations of the girls and young women in your life? Take a moment to reflect on their goals and ambitions. How can you actively invest in and support their dreams to help them flourish?

2. How can you create a nurturing and empowering environment that encourages girls and young women to dream big? What specific actions can you take to provide them with the resources, mentorship, and opportunities they need to pursue their dreams?

3. Consider the long-term impact of investing in the dreams of girls and young women. How can your support and belief in their potential shape their future trajectories and contribute to a more equitable and empowered society? What steps can you take to foster a community that values and invests in the dreams of girls and young women?

Be about It

Discover and support their dreams: Engage in open and supportive conversations with the girls and young women in your life to understand their dreams and aspirations. Take the time to listen and show genuine interest. Once you have a clearer understanding of their goals, actively invest in and support their dreams by offering encouragement, resources, and guidance.

Create a nurturing environment: Foster a supportive and empowering environment that encourages girls and young women to dream big. Provide them with the necessary resources, such as access to education, mentorship, and opportunities, to help them pursue their dreams. Create spaces where they feel safe to express themselves, share their ideas, and receive support from others who believe in their potential.

Be a mentor and seek mentors: Serve as a mentor to girls and young women by offering guidance, sharing insights, and providing encouragement along their journey. Additionally, help them find mentors who can provide valuable support and advice. Connect them with individuals who have expertise in their areas of interest and who can serve as role models and sources of inspiration as they pursue their dreams.

There is freedom waiting

for you, On the breezes

of the sky, And you ask

'What if I fall?'

Oh but my darling,

what if you fly?

—ERIN HANSON

CONCLUSION

What If I Fly?

THERE'S SOMETHING TRULY enchanting about the journey of a caterpillar transforming into a magnificent butterfly. I must confess I stumbled upon this analogy one day while searching for "inspirational metaphors" to share with my athletes after a heartbreaking loss. Little did I know that it would leave a mark on my heart and serve as a constant reminder for both me and my athletes, especially during the toughest of days. The journey of a butterfly resonates deeply because it epitomizes the incredible potential for growth and transformation that lies within each of us.

A butterfly begins as a humble creature with no ability to fly, only to undergo a breathtaking metamorphosis and emerge as an insect capable of soaring thousands of miles. It's a testament to the power of belief and the profound impact of providing support to our girls and young women. When we empower them to dream big and then stand alongside them as they chase those dreams, we witness the extraordinary heights they can reach. This is the power of belief in action.

As I reflect on my own journey, I can honestly say that I am living my dream right now. The joy and fulfillment that come from seeing the incredible growth and accomplishments of the young women I work with are beyond measure. Their resilience, determination, and spirit inspire me to keep pushing forward, even in the face of challenges.

I want you to consider, no matter what role you play in a young girl or woman's life, how are you helping them fly? Are you clipping their wings because you are afraid of where they may go? The reality is that girls and young women have enough to hold them down. It's time that we have people lifting them up. In a world filled with barriers and limitations, we must become the catalysts of change for the girls and young women in our lives. We have the power to ignite their imaginations and instill in them the belief that they can achieve anything they set their minds to. It's not about imposing our own fears and limitations onto them but rather about empowering them to transcend the boundaries that society often places in their way.

Imagine a world where every girl and young woman is encouraged to dream big, where her aspirations are met with encouragement. This is the world we have the opportunity to create. By acknowledging and dismantling the obstacles that already exist, we can pave the way for their dreams to take flight. We can close the dream gap—the space in between young girls' ambition and their potential, hindered not because they are incapable, but by the society they grow up in. It's about fostering an environment where they feel safe to explore their passions, where their ideas are valued, and where they are given the tools and resources to pursue their goals.

Let us be their champions, their allies, and their guiding lights. Let us stand beside them, offering a helping hand when they stumble and celebrating their triumphs along the way. By doing so, we not only uplift their spirits but also inspire others to join the movement, creating a ripple effect of empowerment that extends far beyond our immediate circles.

Together, let us create a society that nurtures and celebrates the dreams of young women. Let us break down the barriers that hinder their progress and create a landscape where their potential knows no bounds. When we invest in their dreams, we invest in a future where equality and empowerment are the cornerstones of our collective success. Be the staircase allowing these girls to climb and reach for the stars.

I implore you to reflect on your role in shaping the dreams of the young women in your life. Are you providing them with the support and encouragement they need to soar? It may require us to confront our own fears and insecurities, but the rewards are immeasurable. By empowering them to overcome obstacles, we not only unlock their individual potential but also contribute to the creation of a world where every young woman has the freedom to explore her full capabilities.

We will be the architects of change, the advocates of dreams, and the catalysts of progress. Together, we can build a future where the aspirations of girls and young women are not only realized but also celebrated as the driving force behind a more inclusive, equitable, and prosperous society. Believe in HER, and watch HER fly.

ACKNOWLEDGMENTS

I am deeply grateful to everyone who encouraged me to write this book.

I am thankful for the support from my husband, Ira, and my boys, Taj and Avi. Your continuous support made this possible.

Thank you Eva Timothy, your painting is a beautiful depiction of helping girls reach for the stars. I hope readers see themselves as the staircase.

Kobe Bryant—thank you for your GIRLdad legacy.

Lastly, to the readers who will dive into the pages of this book, thank you for your curiosity. Your interest in this work fuels my passion for storytelling and sharing my voice with the world.

ABOUT THE AUTHOR

Diljeet Taylor, a resident of Provo, Utah, originally hails from the Central Valley in California. She was raised in a devout Sikh household, with her parents having immigrated from Punjab, India.

With a deep passion for empowering girls and women, Diljeet has dedicated her career to coaching female athletes at the collegiate level for over two decades. Her commitment and expertise have garnered significant recognition, including being honored as the NCAA Coach of the Year in 2021.

Combining her personal experiences and professional achievements, Diljeet brings a unique perspective to her work. Her background and her coaching journey have shaped her understanding of the challenges and potential of girls and women. Diljeet's dedication to empowering individuals shines through her writing, inspiring readers to embrace their strengths and reach their fullest potential.

Her passion for relationships led her to co-found the BYU GIRLdad camp in 2020, a weekend retreat where she is focused on empowering and strengthening the relationship between fathers and their daughters.

Diljeet Taylor's personal and professional journey serves as a testament to her commitment to championing the growth and empowerment of girls and women, making her an influential voice in the field. When she's not helping coach young women on the field, she's busy raising two boys, Taj and Avi, alongside her husband, Ira.

ENDNOTES

1 Logen Breehl and Omar Caban, "Physiology, Puberty," StatPearls, StatPearls Publishing, March 27, 2023, www.ncbi.nlm.nih.gov/books/NBK534827; NeuroRelay, "Female Brain versus Male Brain," October 7, 2012, https://neurorelay.com/2012/10/07/female-brain-versus-male-brain/.

2 Mary M. Heitzeg, Jillian E. Hardee, and Adriene M. Beltz, "Sex Differences in the Developmental Neuroscience of Adolescent Substance Use Risk," *Current Opinion in Behavioral Sciences* 23 (2018): 21.

3 Kimberly M. Albert and Paul A. Newhouse, "Estrogen, Stress, and Depression: Cognitive and Biological Interactions," *Annual Review of Clinical Psychology* 15 (2019): 399.

4 Claire Shipman, Katty Kay, and JillEllyn Riley, "How Puberty Kills Girls' Confidence," *The Atlantic*, September 20, 2018, https://www.theatlantic.com/family/archive/2018/09/puberty-girls-confidence/563804/.

5 K. Kay, C. Shipman, and J. Riley, *The Confidence Code for Girls: Taking Risks, Messing Up, and Becoming Your Amazingly Imperfect, Totally Powerful Self* (New York: HarperCollins, 2018).

6 Mental Health Foundation, *Body Image in Childhood,* 2019, https://www.mentalhealth.org.uk/explore-mental-health/articles/body-image-report-executive-summary/body-image-childhood.

7 Dove, "#KeepHerConfident: Building Body Confidence in Sports," https://www.dove.com/us/en/stories/campaigns/confident-sports.html.

8 K. Kay, C. Shipman, and J. Riley, *The Confidence Code for Girls.*

9 Ypulse, *The Confidence Code for Girls: The Confidence Collapse and Why It Matters for the Next Gen*, 2018, www.confidencecodegirls.com/s/The-Confidence-Code-for-Girls-x-Ypulse.pdf.

10 "Women Rate Themselves as Less Confident Than Men Until Their Mid-40s," Harvard Business Review, https://hbr.org/data-visuals/2019/06/women-rate-themselves-as-less-confident-than-men-until-their-mid-40s.

11 "6 Signs You Have 'Good Girl Syndrome,'" Cleveland Clinic. https://health.clevelandclinic.org/good-girl-syndrome.

12 Gerwig, Greta, director. 2023. *Barbie.* Warner Bros. Pictures. 1 hr., 54 minutes.

13 "New Findings from Teen Survey Shows Beauty Filters Harm Teens' Self-Esteem," ParentsTogether, September 29, 2021, https://parentstogetheraction.org/wp-content/uploads/2021/09/ParentsTogether_Social-Media-Beauty-Filters-Survey-Results_09-29-21.pdf.

14 J. Fardouly, P. C. Diedrichs, L. R. Vartanian, and E. Halliwell, "Social Comparisons on Social Media: The Impact of Facebook on Young Women's Body Image Concerns and Mood," *Body Image* 13 (2015): 38–45.

15 G. Holland and L. Timmerman, "The Influence of Instagram Use on Young Women's Body Image and Mood," *Body Image* 23 (2017): 90–97.

16 A. K. Przybylski, K. Murayama, C. R. DeHaan, and V. Gladwell, "Motivational, Emotional, and Behavioral Correlates of Fear of Missing Out," *Computers in Human Behavior* 29, no. 4 (2013), 1841–1848.

17 Nicole F. Roberts, "Strong Father-Daughter Relationships Lead To Healthier, Happier Women," *Forbes*, June 21, 2020, https://

www.forbes.com/sites/nicolefisher/2020/06/21/strong-father-daughter-relationships-lead-to-healthier-happier-women/.

18 S. R. Jaffee, L. Bowes, I. Ouellet-Morin, H. L. Fisher, T. E. Moffitt, M. T. Merrick, and L. Arseneault, "Safe, Stable, Nurturing Relationships Break the Intergenerational Cycle of Abuse: A Prospective Nationally Representative Cohort of Children in the United Kingdom," *The Journal of Adolescent Health: Official Publication of the Society for Adolescent Medicine* 53, no. S4 (2013): S4–S10.

19 Margo Maine, *Father Hunger: Fathers, Daughters and the Pursuit of Thinness*, 2nd ed. (Nashville: Gurze Books, 2004).

20 Teresa P. Nguyen, Benjamin R. Karney, and Thomas N. Bradbury, "Childhood Abuse and Later Marital Outcomes: Do Partner Characteristics Moderate the Association?" *Journal of Family Psychology* 31, no. 1 (2017): 82; Robert T. Muller, "Trauma Survivors at Risk for Future Abusive Relationships," *Psychology Today*, January 8, 2016, https://www.psychologytoday.com/us/blog/talking-about-trauma/201601/trauma-survivors-risk-future-abusive-relationships.

21 Anna North, "What the Virality of #GirlDad Says about American Fatherhood," Vox (January 31, 2020), https://www.vox.com/2020/1/31/21115318/girldad-dads-daughters-fathers-kobe-bryant.

22 Meg Meeker, *Strong Fathers, Strong Daughters: 10 Secrets Every Father Should Know* (Washington, D.C.: Regnery, 2006).

23 Carol S. Dweck, *Mindset: The New Psychology of Success* (New York: Ballantine Books, 2017).

24 Catherine Good, Joshua Aronson, and Michael Inzlicht, "The Influence of Growth Mindset on Academic Motivation and Resilience for Girls and Boys," *Journal of Youth and Adolescence* 49, no. 5 (2020): 947–959.

25 Gloria Romero and Brent W. Roberts, "Mindset and Women's Career Aspirations: A Meta-analysis," *Personality and Social Psychology Bulletin* 47, no. 2 (2021): 185–204

26 Philip C. Watkins, Kathrane Woodward, Tamara Stone, and Russell L. Kolts, "Gratitude and Happiness: Development of a Measure of Gratitude and Relationships with Subjective Well-Being," *Social Behavior and Personality: An International Journal* 31, no. 5 (2003): 431–452.

27 Andrea Rice, "Rewiring Your Brain for Positivity with 'Mature Gratitude,'" *Psych Central*, accessed November 23, 2021, https://psychcentral.com/health/rewiring-your-brain-for-positivity-with-gratitude.

28 M. Y. Bartlett, P. Valdesolo, and S. N. Arpin, "The Paradox of Power: The Relationship between Self-Esteem and Gratitude," *The Journal of Social Psychology* 160, no. 1 (2020): 27–38.

29 J. K. Rowling, "The Fringe Benefits of Failure, and the Importance of Imagination," speech delivered at Harvard University, Cambridge, MA, June 5, 2008, https://news.harvard.edu/gazette/story/2008/06/text-of-j-k-rowling-speech/.

30 Sam Smith, *There Is No Next: NBA Legends on the Legacy of Michael Jordan* (New York: Diversion Books, 2014).

Made in the USA
Middletown, DE
07 September 2024